SHARING THE
SECRETS
TEACH YOUR
CHILD TO SPELL

SHARING THE SECRETS
TEACH YOUR CHILD TO SPELL

Ruth Scott & Sharon Siamon

Macmillan Canada, Toronto

Canadian Cataloguing in Publication Data

Scott, Ruth
  Sharing the secrets : teach your child to spell

ISBN 0-7715-9044-X

1. English language - Orthography and spelling - Study and teaching (Elementary). I. Siamon, Sharon. II. Title

LB1574.S36 1994   649'.68   C94-931003-4

    3 4 5 98 97 96

Page 43, "The Rain in Spain", words by Alan Jay Lerner. © 1956 by Alan Jay Lerner and Frederick Lowe; © renewed. Chappell & Co. owner of publication and allied rights throughout the world. International Copyright secured. All Rights Reserved. Used by Permission.

Page 97, *Gage Canadian Dictionary*, Walter Avis et al, copyright ©1983 Gage Publishing Limited, used with permission.

Appendix I, *Teaching Spelling* 2nd ed. by Ves Thomas, copyright © 1979 Gage Publishing Limited, used with permission.

Macmillan Canada wishes to thank the Canada Council, the Ontario Ministry of Culture and Communications and the Ontario Arts Council for supporting its publishing program.

Macmillan Canada
A Division of Canada Publishing Corporation
Toronto, Ontario, Canada

Printed in Canada

For Helen

Contents

Preface

For many children, life is full of secrets, and school is no exception: the secrets of long division, of reading new words, of remembering the multiplication tables. It became apparent how mysterious it all seemed when a young boy, who had excelled during his stay at a special learning centre for children with academic problems, explained his success this way—"Here they tell you the secrets." For him the definition of learning was finding out the secrets.

Spelling is a secret that eludes many children and adults. They see words such as **their**, **there**, and **they're** and wonder how they will ever sort them out. They find out there are silent letters in **climb** and **write**, and ask why we can't simply spell the words the way they sound. Worse still, they see some of their friends mastering English spelling, apparently with ease, and they wonder, "What's wrong with me?"

This book is written by two authors who believe that there are secrets of learning to spell that are too exciting to be kept. Ruth Scott and Sharon Siamon are experienced teachers who have written extensively for children and educators. Sharon is an author of many children's books, an accomplished editor, and a co-author of a series of spelling textbooks used throughout Canada. She is also a popular guest author in many schools, where she discusses her writing and encourages students to develop their writing talents.

Ruth Scott is an assistant professor in the Faculty of Education at Brock University in St. Catharines, Ontario. Ruth, whose doctorate is based on the links between spelling and reading, has authored and co-authored seven books on spelling, and has lectured to teachers and parents in every Canadian province. Her articles have appeared in academic journals, teacher publications, and national newspapers.

Most important, perhaps, both Sharon and Ruth are parents of school-aged children. They readily admit to having both strong and weak spellers in their families, and share the concerns of all parents when their children seem to be lagging behind in spelling development.

This book is Ruth Scott and Sharon Siamon's attempt to "share the secrets" of learning to spell. It is for parents, teachers, grandparents, friends—anyone who wishes to help a child become a better speller. One of the secrets that you may discover is that by helping someone else learn to spell, you, too, will become a better speller! This is a secret too good to keep!

Getting Started

English spelling has not changed much since you went to school. It is true the English language is always adding new words, but compared to science or mathematics it is a limited, stable body of information. What has changed is our understanding of the spelling system and how children learn to spell.

On the one hand, English spelling may seem very confusing and unpredictable. For example, look at this simple counting rhyme, based on some of the most important words in the English language, the numbers one to ten.

One, **two**,
buckle my **shoe**.

Three, **four**,
shut the **door**.

Five, **six**,
Pick up **sticks**.

Seven, **eight**,
Lay them **straight**.

Nine, **ten**,
A big fat **hen**!

Look at the rhyming words **two—shoe, four—door, six—sticks, eight—straight**. Not until we get to the last couplet are rhyming words spelled with the same letters, **ten—hen**. Why? Because there are many ways to spell the same sound in English.

English spelling is not based on a simple match between letters and sounds, as in languages such as Italian. Our written language has never been rigidly codified, and in the past, printers and scribes spelled according to their preference, or even according to the length of the line. English is also a language that is ever-changing, and welcoming words from a variety of sources. Thus we have **fax**, a new short form for **facsimile** (and fortunately, a much easier one to spell!). We also welcome words such as **taco** and **panzarotti** from other languages which do not have the same spelling system as our own.

However complicated this makes our written language, it is not impossible to learn to spell. Look back at the counting rhyme. Almost 70% or 18 out of 26 words follow regular phonics rules that you will find in Section 1 of this program: **buckle, my, three, shut, five, six, pick, up, sticks, seven, lay, them, nine, ten, a, big, fat, hen**.

It is true that these are all fairly simple words. How about the real toughies, words such as **Wednesday, February,** or **minute**? These three words are hard, but important. A child who can't spell them by the end of elementary school is going to appear poorly educated. There are many such words in English, as well as thousands of regular words, so how does your child go about learning to spell?

Learn the Most Commonly Written Words

Before you throw up your hands, take comfort in the fact that if your child learns a core of about 200 high-frequency words he or she can spell almost sixty percent of the words needed for the common, everyday tasks of writing. **Four** and **eight**, trickier words from the nursery rhyme above, are words your child will use very often. He or she will probably learn them by sight. However, not all children learn to spell words just by seeing them frequently. It makes sense to learn the basic list of 200 words most commonly used, as well as a list of most commonly **misspelled** words. These words often do not follow common spelling patterns and must be memorized.

Both of these lists are found in Appendix I, page 139. As well, we have integrated these essential words into the unit lists, so that your child will get constant practice writing them.

Learn the Simple, Essential Patterns of English Spelling

The second way to help your child become a good speller is to teach the basic patterns of language until they are second nature. Although it is true many English words break the rules, the majority follow them. In teaching these patterns, the book starts in Sections 1,2, and 3 with the simple rhyming families (**cat—hat, run—sun**) and talks about the building blocks of language—the vowels and consonants, showing how words fall into spelling patterns according to how these vowels and consonants are arranged.

If your child is beyond third grade, but has missed the simple beginning patterns, it will be worthwhile to take her or him through Sections 1,2, and 3, just to make sure the common patterns are in place.

Once your child has learned the patterns at the basic level, Section 4 will show how to build simple compound words such as **sunshine**. Also in Section 4, patterns for adding endings such as **ing** and **ed** are introduced. Suddenly, the written language explodes for your child, as he or she gains command of how to expand the words already mastered. By the end of Section 4, your child will be able to extend **rain** into such forms as **rainy**, **rains**, **rained**, **raining**, **rainbow**, **raincoat**, **raindrop**, and **rainfall**.

Finally, because English is English, children will need to learn tactics for remembering the spelling of longer and harder words. In Section 5, your child will learn how to use meaning connections—the word **sign**, for example, is related to the words **signal**, **signature**, and **significant**, which explains the presence of the silent **g**. As well in Section 5, other suffixes and prefixes are added to words, and words that come from other languages are discussed. Section 6 focuses on special spelling challenges, including difficult vowel sounds, harder word pairs such as **picture** and **pitcher**, and misleading pronunciations in words such as **February**. These challenges are met by having children develop tactics for remembering the tricky features. They can remember the shape of a word such as **which**, exaggerate the **d** and **nes** in Wednesday instead of saying *Wensday*, or develop memory tricks such as "I can spell **friend**—it's a fri**end** to the **end**." At all levels we suggest tactics your child can use to remember harder words, but in Section 6, these "secrets" get special emphasis.

From Parent to Teacher

You may have some concerns about becoming a teacher for your child. "What do I know about teaching someone to spell? I still make spelling errors myself!" or "What can I do that is not already being done at school?"

Keep in mind that you have been your child's teacher for many years already. You know your child's temperament and the best ways to encourage him or her. Through this program you will be able to give the individual attention that teachers at school wish they had time to provide.

Although teaching spelling seems very different from teaching your child to walk or talk, in many ways it is not. Did you expect your child to move effortlessly from learning to say "car" and "dog" to speaking in full sentences? Of course not. You understood that spoken language develops over a period of years, and that each step forward involves taking a risk, making mistakes, practising, and then moving on again. You celebrated each new word or phrase, but did not scold your child for saying, "I goed outside yesterday." You probably repeated the correct form in a natural way, "You **went** outside, did you?" knowing that the proper form would soon take hold.

15 minutes of spelling practice a day is the maximum time recommended. Consider using a timer to ensure that sessions don't run too long.

In the same way, a child can't learn to spell in one or two sessions. The length of time it takes to go through this program will vary with each child, according to age, word awareness, and many other factors. The important thing is to encourage your child's progress and to make the experience a positive one. One way of doing this is to keep the daily time periods short. Hours of drill will achieve nothing but frustration and rebellion. **Fifteen minutes a day is ideal.**

What is smarter than a talking dog? A spelling bee!

Besides formal practice, children need **word focus** to become competent spellers, and this can go on any time of the day. Focus on words your child likes—dinosaur words or food words. Focus on words **as words**—the way they look, sound, feel (when you trace them on each other's back, or make them out of Plasticine). Discuss the meaning of words and have fun making riddles, puns, and jokes from them. Look at words in comic strips, on labels, on road signs, on licence plates. Become a family of word detectives, searching for new and interesting words and spellings.

And finally, encourage your child to write as often as possible with a real purpose for communicating. It could be a set of rules for a game, badges for a club, posters for an event, a note for the family, or a card for a friend. When your child writes, encourage a consciousness of spelling correctness. If a first draft is necessary to get the ideas down, encourage a second or final draft where the spelling is proofread and correctness is the goal.

These activities will help your child not only improve his or her spelling skills, but develop a spelling "conscience," so that proofreading, looking up words he or she is uncertain about, and correcting written material will become a habit. Proofreading and rewriting skills are simply part of the spelling and writing process and it's important that your child understands this.

How Children Learn to Spell

While spelling itself may not have changed much in the past few decades, great progress has been made in understanding how children learn to spell. We now know that spelling development is systematic even though children may vary in the rate at which they learn to spell. As you become aware of some of the stages children pass through in spelling you will be able to look at your child's spelling in a different way.

Research has shown that most children begin writing by scribbling. They make marks that look like writing on whatever surface is available.

Often by the time children are in kindergarten they attempt to write letters, sometimes the letters they associate with their own names. They are not fussy about the order, or whether the letters are capitals or small letters. The first letters written are letters like **R**, **T**, **S**, **B**—consonants that have the most definite and recognizable sounds.

Not until later will children attempt to write words, or groups of words in sentences. And when they first add vowel sounds (**a**, **e**, **i**, **o**, **u**) to words, they are not particular about which vowel sound, or they may try to use the letter name: **bi** for **by**.

Throughout the early school years children gradually learn to spell short vowels correctly, as in **bet**, **bat**, **bit**, and **but**. Often by the second or third grade, they begin to see that long vowel sounds can be spelled in a number of ways, as in **go**, **flow**, **coat**, and **mope**. It takes some time before they can remember which pattern is correct for which word, but this is still a great step beyond spelling **boat** as simply **bot**.

As children enter the middle grades, they begin to move beyond just sounding words out. With proper instruction, they are now able to understand some of the rules for adding endings to words, making words plural, forming contractions, and so forth. They also realize that longer words are often formed by adding prefixes and suffixes to shorter words, as in the case of **international** (inter + nation + al). This understanding goes hand-in-hand with their growing vocabularies and reading skills.

Spelling growth does not end with the beginning of high school. On the contrary, your child will continue to learn new things about English spelling throughout his or her life. Even very good spellers need to learn tactics for the many words in English with special challenges—silent letters, double consonants, confusing pronunciations, unusual origins, and so forth.

Naturally, you are not expected to know all these rules and patterns yourself! That is what this book is for. We have organized the program so that it follows the normal stages of growth that research tells us most children follow. It will give your child just the right amount of support to go along with what he or she may be picking up from reading or from instruction in school. By using the program with your child, you can ensure that there are no major gaps in his or her understanding of the spelling system.

Just as you would not expect a three-year-old to perform complicated gymnastic routines, you should also realize that your child may reach a point in the program where he or she can't go any further for the time being. This is the time to put the book away and come back to it in a few weeks or months. You may be surprised to find that your child has matured enough to understand the next stages of the program that seemed so difficult just a few months before. One of the big "secrets" of this book is to make it work for your child, not the other way around.

How to Use This Program

Equipment you will need

The program can be carried out with basic supplies that you likely already have at home: pencils, eraser, a three-ring notebook, lined paper. A dictionary is also an important resource. The dictionary we have used in the preparation of the book is the *Gage Canadian Dictionary*. For younger children you may wish to try a good picture dictionary.

Be sure to keep all supplies together so that the time you spend on the program can be used most productively.

The structure of the program

Sharing the Secrets has six major sections:

Section 1: Short Vowels
Section 2: Long Vowels
Section 3: Other Vowel Patterns
Section 4: Word Building
Section 5: Meaning Connections
Section 6: Special Challenges

Each section contains a number of individual units that follow a similar format. The average unit is designed to last about four sessions of fifteen minutes each. In this way, you can expect to cover at least a unit each week. Don't worry, however, if your child takes a shorter or longer time to complete a unit—these are only suggested times.

Below is a description of the sections of each unit and how they may fit into a four-day schedule:

Day One

Pretest: Dictate the Unit Words and Challenge Words without having your child study them beforehand. Say the word, use it in a sentence, then say it again. For example: **jump** Can you **jump** this high? **jump**. If you prefer to use the dictation sentences already prepared, you will find them shown opposite the word list; however, don't hesitate to improvise.

Have your child print the words (not the sentences) in his or her notebook or on the special dictation form found on the last page. You are free to photocopy this form and use it with each unit.

Now mark the Pretest with your child. Have him or her recopy correctly any misspelled words, paying special attention to the letters that caused difficulty. These letters could be highlighted with a special colour of ink or with a highlighter pen. The Challenge Words usually follow the pattern or rule for the unit, but as the name suggests, are more difficult than the words in the Unit list.

A sample dictation sheet is shown below:

dictation	rewrite	posttest
wile	while	
pris	prize	

If your child has no errors on the Pretest, you might wish to skip the unit and go on to the next. It may be worthwhile, however, to discuss the "Spelling Secret" for the unit so that your child can apply it to more challenging words.

"What's the Secret?": Guide your child through the questions and activities leading up to the "Spelling Secret" for the unit. This section is very important since it will help your child to notice patterns rather than just try to memorize a rule.

"Spelling Secret": These sentences summarize the rule or pattern that fits most of the words in the unit. If your child does not understand the rule, try reviewing the activities in "What's the Secret?"

Day Two
Review the **"Spelling Secret"** from the previous day with your child.
"Putting the Secret to Work": Begin work on the activities that follow the Secret. These exercises focus on using the spelling pattern or rule described in the **"Spelling Secret"** for the unit.

Day Three
Complete **"Putting the Secret to Work."**

Day Four
Posttest: Dictate the Unit and Challenge Words again. If you are using the Dictation Form provided on the back page, have your child fold over the Pretest section and print the words under the Posttest column. Mark the Posttest, having your child rewrite correctly any misspelled words. Keep a list of these difficult words in a special place in the spelling binder so that you can review these words often.

It is important to note how your child has improved from the Pretest—you may even decide to use a simple graph to show the change between the first and second unit tests. Do not emphasize how far your child is from perfection, but how much improvement has occurred. This will help to create a positive feeling and encourage him or her to continue to grow in spelling.

"Home Connections": Do any of the optional activities suggested in the "Home Connections" throughout the week.

You may also wish to look in Appendix II for other words that fit the pattern or rule for this unit. For example, page 146 contains a list of contractions in addition to those covered in Unit 30.

Where to Begin?
Most children will probably not need to begin this program at Unit 1. Show your child the book, explain how it is organized, and decide together which unit to choose as a starting point. Your child's performance on the Pretest should be a good clue to you. If several errors are made, it may be too advanced a level, and you should backtrack to an earlier unit. On the other hand, if your child has every word correct, you might want to move ahead to a more advanced level.

We hope that both you and your child will find this program useful. You may find that there are units you wish to work on yourself to advance your own spelling skills. Don't be bashful about doing this! Children need to know that becoming a good speller is a life-long process and that it is all right to admit to spelling difficulties. Have fun!

1 Short Vowels

Short Vowels

Introduction

At five and six, most children begin to write. They soon make the connection between the sounds we make and the marks we make on paper, and they too want to capture the magic of the spoken word by writing it down.

In Section 1 your child will learn to spell the most basic words. These are grouped in Word Families to make them easier to learn and remember. Many children can hear that **mat** rhymes with **sat**, **fat**, and **cat**, but do not understand the connection between sound and spelling. When they learn that the words in each family not only sound the same at the end, but look the same, they have a powerful key for unlocking the spelling of countless words.

The best place to begin teaching your child to spell is with the 26 letters of our English alphabet. Five are vowels: **a, e, i, o, u**; the other 21 letters are consonants. The letter **y** is tricky. It can be a consonant in **yes**, but it is a vowel in **baby**, where it is pronounced as an *e*.

Consonants: Children usually write consonants before they attempt to put vowels in words. **Love** is often spelled **lv** and **monster** as **mstr**. Consonants generally have only one sound, and although a child may not hear them all at first, they provide powerful clues for spelling words.

It's very important that your child can hear the difference between consonant sounds, especially those that are close, such as **b** and **p**, **d** and **t**, **m** and **n**. You will find exercises in Section 1 that help your child hear the consonants by comparing words such as **bat** and **pat**.

Vowels: The five vowels can be slippery characters! Each vowel in English has two main sounds that we call long and short.

The long version of the vowels sounds like the letter names: *a* in **ate**, *e* in **eat**, *i* in **ivy**, *o* in **open**, and *u* in **use**. The short vowels are the sounds you hear in short words such as **pat, bet, bit, pot, but.**

In Section 1 we begin with words with one short vowel sound. We have started with one syllable words so that your child can focus on the basic patterns of English spelling:
- one vowel + one consonant (**at, in, up**);
- one consonant + one vowel + one consonant (**cat, win, cup**);
- consonants + one vowel + consonants (**frog, kick, thank**).

Challenge Words: Fortunately, a majority of the 200 most frequently written words follow predictable patterns. At the same time, there are many frequently written words such as **one** and **said** that do not fit patterns. We need a special focus to learn these words, and so have grouped them as **Challenge Words**. In both **Unit** and **Challenge Word** lists we have starred the 25 most frequently misspelled for you so they can be given special attention.

Rhyme is an important tool in learning to spell. Children who are good spellers know that if **tip** rhymes with **sip**, chances are the last two letters will be the same.

The difference between vowel and consonant sounds lies in the way we produce them. A vowel is a speech sound in which our vocal cords vibrate and the breath is not blocked by our tongue, teeth or lips. A consonant is produced by partly or completely blocking the breath. (Say **a** and then **b** to feel the difference.)

Several consonants have two sounds. For example:
- hard *g* as in **garden**, and soft *g* as in **gem**.
- soft *c* as in **city** and hard *c* as in **cook.**
- *s* as in **sip** or *s* as in **as.**

Your child can learn to recognize the number of syllables in words by putting her hand under her chin as she says them slowly. Each time she makes a vowel sound her jaw drops a little. She can feel the number of syllables in a word by leaving her hand under her jaw as she says **birthday, lunch,** or **Saturday.**

A note of caution. If many letters or words are misspelled in the early units, don't push. Reinforce the letter-sound connection by:

• reading alphabet books that are fun, such as *A Wildlife ABC*★ with your child;

• reading simple poetry out loud to help your child develop a sense of rhyme. Try *The Random House Book of Poetry*★ or Dennis Lee's *Alligator Pie*★;

• writing letters to match the sounds heard at the beginning of familiar words such as your child's name or household objects. Ask "What's the sound you hear at the beginning of your name? Which letter makes that sound?";

• making word cards to help your child learn the relationship between sounds and letters. For example, print a **b** (capital and small letter) on a card and paste or draw a picture of a ball beside it. Print the word **ball** on the other side of the card.

Practise with word cards for a few days or weeks until your child is more confident. Once the sound-letter connection is more solid, you can begin Section 1 again.

References

★*A Wildlife ABC*, Jan Thornhill, Greey de Pencier, 1984

★*A Northern Alphabet*, Ted Harrison, Tundra Books, 1987

★*Alligator Pie*, Dennis Lee, Macmillan Canada, 1974

★*The Random House Book of Poetry for Children*, selected by Jack Prelutsky, Random House, 1983

UNIT 1

Letters and Sounds

When doing the spelling test, it's helpful to use a three column format such as the one shown on the back page. The words for the first dictation should be written in the first column.

Dictate the Unit Words. Say each word clearly, read the sentence and repeat the word. For example: **dog**—Our **dog** is brown and white.—**dog**

Unit Words

bag	The children gathered around the mysterious **bag.**
cat	Jane loves the way her **cat** purrs.
dog	Our **dog** is brown and white.
fish	The **fish** at the end of Lisa's line was huge!
gum	His bubble burst and the **gum** stuck all over his face.
hop	That frog can **hop** a long way!
jet	It was Jenny's first time on a **jet.**
kick	She could **kick** the ball farther than anyone.
leg	When Jeff broke his **leg** he had to use crutches.
mug	Sara's sister would drink only out of her blue **mug.**
net	They caught the big fish in a **net.**
pig	Mike brought a **pig** to school for show and tell.
quit	They didn't want to **quit** until they finished the game.

red   Pete was so mad his face turned as **red** as a racing car.

six   All **six** of them crept up to the house.

ten   Chris has saved **ten** dollars.

van   The Smith's new car is a grey **van**.

web   The spider's **web** was covered in dew.

yes   Nodding your head means "**yes**."

zip   I have to **zip** up my coat before I go out.

> If you use the three column format, use the third one to re-do the test after completing the unit. Simply fold the first two columns over to hide the words.

Rewrite any misspelled words in the second column.

dictation	rewrite	posttest
wed	web	

What's the Secret?

1. Circle the letters a, e, i, o, u in the words below. We call these letters vowels. Say the words out loud and listen to the vowel sounds.

     bag   **cat**   **dog**   **net**   **pig**   **gum**

Write the word **quit** and circle the vowels. The letter **q** is always followed by **u,** to make the consonant sound *q*: **q__ __ t**

> Your child should be clear that the *sound* of the letter is different from the letter name. For example, are they hearing *ssss* at the beginning of **six**? (You can tell them it's the sound a snake makes!)

2. All the other letters in the alphabet are called consonants. Underline the consonants in the words below. Say the words out loud and listen to the consonant sounds at the beginning and end.

     bag   **hop**   **jet**   **leg**   **red**   **six**   **van**   **web**   **zip**

Spelling Secret #1

Our English alphabet has 26 letters. Five are vowels and the rest are consonants. Every English word has at least one vowel in it. The spelling pattern **consonant–vowel–consonant** is common: **bag cat dog**

Putting the Secret to Work

1. Complete this sentence:

     Our alphabet has _____letters. We have _____vowels and _____ consonants.

> The long vowels say the letter names, as in the alphabet: A, E, I, O, U. The short vowels need to be learned as separate sounds. Associate them with familiar objects or animals (e.g., **a** as in apple, **i** as in igloo, **e** as in elephant, **o** as in octopus, **u** as in umbrella).

2. Write the letter that spells the sound you hear at the beginning of each picture word below.

__pple   __mbrella   __lephant   __ctopus   __gloo

3. Say the words in the chart out loud. What sound does each vowel have? We call these sounds the *short vowel sounds*.

a	e	i	o	u
bag	jet	fish	dog	gum
cat	leg	kick	hop	mug

4. Put the letter **b** in front of these word endings. Sound out the words you have made.

*b*at   ___it   ___in   ___ox

5. Put the letter **t** in front of these endings. Write the words you have made.

__in   ___an   ___ot

6. Add the letter **p** to these endings. Read the sentences.

I have a ___*et* raccoon. I keep him in a ___*en*. I can ___*at* him and feed him from my hand!

7. Word Search. Find a word beginning with each consonant and vowel in this puzzle. You can go in any direction and use letters in more than one word.

at	lick	win
bun	man	X-ray
cot	not	yet
did	on	zoo
end	pup	
fun	quit	
got	rib	
hay	sob	
it	top	
jet	up	
kick	vat	

X	r	a	y	f	s	g	o	m	s	q
k	i	c	k	u	o	n	m	i	g	u
n	b	u	n	n	b	y	a	h	o	i
p	u	p	o	t	g	e	n	a	t	t
t	c	o	t	e	n	t	u	y	d	d
a	w	i	n	l	l	i	c	k	n	i
v	o	o	z	f	t	e	j	m	e	d

8. Make new words by changing the consonant at the end to an **n**.

gu*m*   ta*b*   ru*b*   su*b*   ma*p*

gu*n*   ___   ___   ___   ___

9. Make new words by changing the consonant at the beginning of each word to an **s**.

*f*un   *w*it   *f*at   *t*ip   *g*et

*s*un   ___   ___   ___   ___

10. Many words end in consonant combinations that make one sound. Read the word **fish**. What sound do you hear at the end? Complete these words with the letters **sh**. Say the words you have written.

di___   ra___   wi___   ru___

The letters **ck** often spell the *k* sound at the end of a word, but never at the beginning. Patterns like this are called *positional constraints*.

11. The letters **ck** at the end of a word also make one sound, the *k* sound in **kick**. Complete these words by adding **ck**. Sound out the words you have made.

ro___   pi___   lu___   ne___

Home Connections

There are many ways to reinforce letter-sound connections throughout the day. For example, you can keep a set of magnetic letters on the refrigerator door and have children look for the letter that begins or ends a word you call out. Letters in alphabet soup, noodles, or cereal can all help sound recognition. (e.g., "Look for the letter that makes the sound that you hear at the beginning of the word **rabbit**.")

Younger children can enjoy making letters out of Play-Doh ™, Plasticine, or cookie dough. Always reinforce the sound of the letter as well as the letter name (e.g., "What sound does the letter **d** make?).

To teach the short vowel sounds use picture dictionaries and alphabet books that show both the letter names and the short sounds. "A is for apple, ant, and alligator." Help your child hear the short vowel sounds in the middle of words by sounding them out carefully: **b-a-t**.

UNIT 2

Dictate the Unit and Challenge Words, using the sentences below or your own sentences.

Word Families with *g*, *b*, and *t*

Unit Words

it	"I found **it**!" Lindsay yelled.
at	He is **at** home.
big	She wanted to open her **big** present last.
got	Joe **got** a new bike.
job	My sister has a **job** at the bakery.
but	His birthday party was fun **but** too short.
get	Tim went to **get** his third piece of cake.
not	The evil king would **not** let the prince go.
hit	Emma's big **hit** won the baseball game.
met	I **met** her at a party.
lot	There has been a **lot** of rain lately.
cab	We called a **cab** to take us to the airport.
hug	She gave her grandmother a big **hug** and a kiss.
shot	He **shot** his arrow at the target.
frog	The princess turned the **frog** into a prince.

Challenge Words

the	What in **the** world happened here?
that	**That** was a funny thing to do!
what	She remembered **what** she was going to say.
flag	The **flag** flew from the top of the flagpole.
scrub	You need to **scrub** the pot with soap.

Check the Pretest with your child.

Rewrite any misspelled words and underline the difficult letter or letters.

<u>fr</u> o g

What's the Secret?

1. Say these words out loud. What part of each word *sounds* the same?

fat   cat   hat

We say these words *rhyme.*

2. Write these words and circle the part that *looks* the same.

mat   sat   bat

We say that **mat, sat, bat, fat,** and **cat** are in the same Word Family because they rhyme and are spelled the same at the end.

3. Say these words and look at them carefully. Are they a Word Family? Why?

hug   bug   rug   tug

Spelling Secret #2

Grouping short words into rhyming families can help us spell them. Many large, easy Word Families end in a vowel and the letters **b, g,** or **t**: **job, sob, rob; hug, mug, tug; get, net, wet**.

Putting the Secret to Work

Word Families that end in *t*

1. The Word Families that end in **t** are especially large and useful. Write all the words that you can make using the wheels below.

Make sure your child can say each word clearly. Sometimes spelling problems occur because a child is not hearing and pronouncing a word accurately.

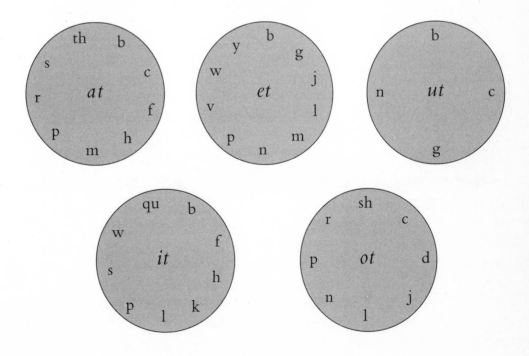

2. Which words rhyme? Only one pair of words in each list rhymes. Write the words and underline the rhyming parts.   f a t—c a t

cat—cab	pet—pen	but—bat	pot—cot
mat—met	pet—get	bet—bit	pit—pot
fat—cat	wet—wit	but—cut	fit—fat

Sh, **wh**, and **th** are examples of what we call consonant *digraphs or blends*. You can say that *sh* is the sound we make when we want someone to be quiet (Shh!).

3. Sometimes two consonants are squished together to make a new sound. For example: **s + h** makes **sh**. Write the *sh* words to match these clues.

To close a window   s h <u>u t</u>
a boat that can sail the ocean   s h __ __
to look for something in a store   s h __ __
the front of your leg   s h __ __

4. Solve these Word Family rhyming riddles!
An overfed rodent is a __at __at.
An aircraft in the rain is a __et __et.
A very warm saucepan is a __ot __ot.
What you get when an elephant sits on your baseball cap is a __ __at __at!

Word Families that end in *g*

5. Make rhyming words that end in **g** by joining the consonants on the outside of the bubbles with the endings in the middle.

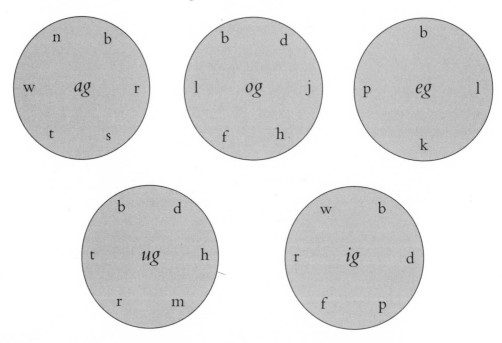

6. Which words rhyme? Write the rhyming pair in each list below.
Underline the part that rhymes: **d <u>o g</u> —f r <u>o g</u>**

bag—bug	beg—bet	wag—wig	smug—smog
dig—dog	beg—leg	mug—Meg	Bob—bog
dog—frog	rig—rip	rug—tug	rag—bag

7. Some consonants can be blended together to make one sound. Write the Unit Word that begins with the sound of **f + r:** *fr__ __*
Write the Challenge Word that begins with the sound of **f + l:** *fl__ __*

Word Families that end with *b*

8. Write the Unit and Challenge Words that rhyme with the words below.
    sob, mob, rob, _____
    jab, lab, tab, _____
    cub, rub, tub, _____
Sometimes three consonants squish together to make one sound: **s + c + r** makes the sound you hear at the beginning of the Challenge Word **scrub.**

9. Which words rhyme? Write each pair of rhyming words and underline the part that rhymes.

job—log	bib—bob	rib—crib	rib—rob
sob—rob	cab—cat	job—jab	lab—lad
cab—cad	cub—rub	hub—hut	sub—club

10. The is the word most often written in our language. Count how many times you can find **the** on this page. _____
Write the two Challenge Words that start with **th** and have the shapes below.

11. Write the Challenge Word that begins with **wh**.
    wh__ __
Notice that the **a** in **what** sounds like short *o* or short *u* (depending on your accent). How can you remember the **a?** Try a silly rhyme.
    A big fat cat
    Sat upon my hat.
    What do you think of that!

Home Connection

If your child has difficulty recognizing rhyming pairs, practise with:
• more pairs like those in exercises 5, 7, and 10. See Appendix II for more samples;
• reading rhyming prose and poetry out loud;
• giving your child a word and asking her to give you back a word that rhymes: **job—Bob**;
• examining the rhyming parts of the words visually, **rib—crib,** so that they can see it is the vowel plus the final consonant that rhymes in each word.

When writing rhyming words, notice which parts, if any, are confusing your child. Is it the vowels (**r**i**b, r**o**b**) or final consonants (ca**b,** ca**d**)? Lots of practice with Dr. Seuss books, *Berenstein Bears, Madeline* books, or any rhyming poems or stories will help children learn to hear the final rhyming sounds (**cab—gab**).

Dictate the Unit and Challenge Words. Use sentences such as those below to help make the meaning clear.

Word Families with *d* and *m*
Words that end in *s*

Unit Words

as

am

is

has

had

did

Mom

Dad

him

his

bed

us

mud

this

a

He was dressed **as** a pirate for the costume party.

I **am** so cold without my warm coat!

Is your dad coming with us?

Maria **has** to get her hair cut today.

She **had** to walk her dog yesterday.

What **did** you do on the holidays?

Mom loves to garden.

Dad loves to cook.

We sneaked **him** in through the back way.

His home was so big and beautiful.

The **bed** was soft and comfortable.

If you come with **us** you are sure to have fun.

I had thick black **mud** all over my shoes.

I hope **this** shirt fits!

Grandfather took **a** poker and stirred the fire.

Challenge Words

said★

them

from

does

was

She **said** she needed to go shopping.

Without **them** we couldn't go.

He has just moved here **from** France.

Does your dog like to play fetch?

Nura **was** on her way to school.

★One of the 25 most frequently misspelled words

Encourage your child to pay special attention to the parts of words he misspelled as you check the Pretest together.

Rewrite any misspelled words. Practise words such as **does** and **said** by writing them with blanks for the hard letters.

d__ __ s   s __ __ d

What's the Secret?

1. Say these pairs of words out loud. Listen for the rhyme. Underline or circle the rhyming parts.

had—dad   am—ham   us–bus

2. Say this pair of rhyming words. Listen for the **s** sound at the end. Is it the same as the sound at the end of **bus**? What sound do you hear?

as—has

Spelling Secret #3

Many short words can be grouped in families that end in **m** or **d**:

had—dad   hid—did   am–Sam

The double **ss** always has the sound of *s*. Word families that end in **ass**, **ess**, **iss**, **oss**, and **uss** are taught in Unit 6.

The blends **gl** and **sl** are used at the beginning of words such as **glad** and **slid**. Sometimes children need a little practice to hear the second sound. Help them by emphasizing the **l** in words such as **slip**, **slap**, **sled**, and **slid**.

The letter **s** has two sounds at the end of words: *z* and *s*:   **as** **us**

Putting the Secret to Work

Word Families that end in *d*

1. Make as many words as you can from the wheels. The words will end in a short vowel + **d**. The **ad** family is one of the biggest and most important short vowel patterns.

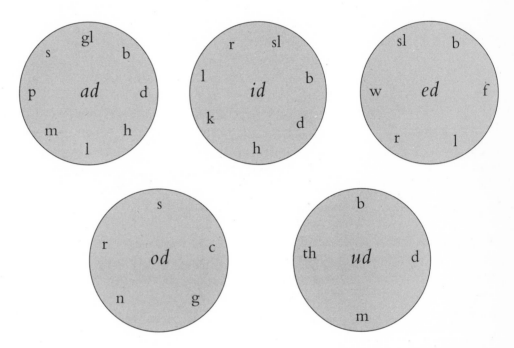

2. Write the pairs of rhyming words from the circles above that answer these riddles.

A flower that didn't bloom is a **dud bud**!

A happy father is a ____ ____.

An angry boy is a ____ ____.

3. Write the Challenge Word that rhymes with **red**, but is spelled with the vowels **ai**.

"This is one of the hardest words to spell!" he __ __ __ __.

4. Which words rhyme? Write the pairs of words that rhyme in the lists below.

bad—dad	cod—cot	nod—sod	mad—met
rod—rid	bed—fed	had—hid	bud—mud
bud—but	lad—lid	hat—kid	dad—did

Word Families with *m*

5. Complete the triangles with words that end in a short vowel + **m**.

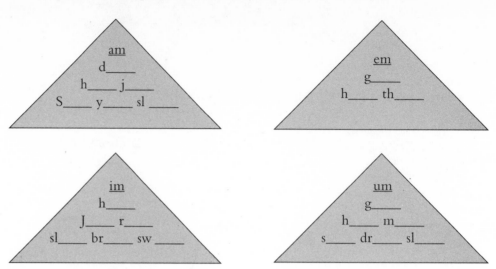

6. Write the Challenge Word that rhymes with **hum** but doesn't fit the pattern.
   She lives a long way **fr__ __** here.

7. Mom and **Mum** are short forms of **mother**. Both spellings are correct. We put a capital letter on **mom** and **dad** when they stand for a person's name.
   For example:
   I know **Mom** likes apples.
   I look like my **mom**.
Write the word correctly in these sentences.
   I like to work with my _____. (Dad, dad)
   Her ____ has to work late. (Mom, mom)
   I'll ask ____ for the number. (Dad, dad)
   We'll see if ____ knows where it is. (Mom, mom)
   "_____, can you come here?" Lee shouted. (Dad, dad)

8. Write the Challenge Word that rhymes with *hem*
   th__ __

Words that end in *s*

9. Write each word in the correct column:
   us, was, gas, as, this, has, his, yes, does, is

ends with the sound *s* as in see	ends with the sound *z* as in zip
us	was

10. Write the Unit and Challenge Words that end in **s** in these sentences about Jack and the Beanstalk (a word may be used more than once).

as   is   has   his   us   this   does   was

Jack __ __ __ a poor boy. But he was __ __ brave __ __ a lion. He said, "I will plant __ __ __ __ bean and see what happens."

__ __ __ mom said, "That __ __ a tall beanstalk. Where __ __ __ __ it go?"

Jack said, "It __ __ __ to go somewhere. I'll climb it and see. Maybe a fortune is waiting for __ __ at the top."

Exercise 11 can be used to check whether your child can hear and spell the short vowel sounds.

11. Write the word that matches each picture below.

b__t   b__s   b__d   k__d   l__g   j__m

Home Connections

To practise short vowel combinations, you might want to make a set of cards. These could include:

• several cards for each consonant;

• several for each of the short vowel Word Family endings: **at, ip, um,** and so on. Use the word wheels in this unit's exercises to find more. Encourage your child to use the cards to make words such as **bat**, and **sip**. You could add cards for consonant combinations **sh, fl, gl,** and **fr.**

Use the cards to play games:

• match my rhyming word;

• make as many rhyming words as you can.

Suppose your child wants to know which words with the *k* sound start with **k** as in **kid**. Take a look in a good young people's dictionary such as *The Gage Junior Dictionary.*

Dictionary skills—Alphabetical Order

Ask your child:

Where does **c** come in the alphabet? Where will you find it in the dictionary? Will it be near the beginning, middle, or end of the book?

Show them that the words are arranged alphabetically. The letter **c** comes after **b** and before **d**. In the same way all the words beginning with **k** come after _____ and before _____.

You can point out that there are many more words that begin with **c** than **k**. Words with the *k* sound followed by a short **i** or short **e** usually start with **k**. The important ones for them to learn are: **key, keep, kick, kid, kill, king, kiss,** and **kitchen.** They may also be interested in words such as **kangaroo** that come from another language.

Dictate the Unit and Challenge Words. Be sure to say the words clearly.

Word Families with *n*, *p*, and *x*

Unit Words

an	She looked up and saw **an** airplane.
in	The kitten cried at the door, wanting **in**.
can	She opened a **can** of tuna for the wet cat.
on	He flipped around the channels to see what was **on** TV.
up	She climbed **up** and **up** until she reached the top.
man	There was a **man** behind the counter in the pet store.
upon★	**Upon** his shoulder there was a parrot.
men	They sat and watched the **men** play basketball.
fix	Her dad taught her to **fix** anything.
ran	The dog **ran** after the ball.
top	I want to be on **top** of the pyramid!
fun	As soon as school is over, I'm going to have **fun**!
ship	Jodi went to the island on a cruise **ship**.
run	Maria could always **run** the fastest and win the races.
box	Nick got a big **box** in the mail.

Challenge Words

one	He grabbed **one** of the cookies off the plate.
than	His hand was quicker **than** lightning.
when★	His mother saw him **when** she came into the kitchen.
then	She smiled, **then** put the cookies away.
seven	She didn't know he had already eaten **seven** cookies.

★One of the 25 most frequently misspelled words

Check the Pretest. Focus on the letters your child has spelled correctly (the part she knows) as well as the problem areas (the part she needs to learn).

Rewrite any words that were misspelled.

What's the Secret?

1. Make three columns like the ones below. Write the following Unit Words under the correct heading: **an, ship, box, run, fix, fun, up, man, six, top.**

words ending in **n**	words ending in **p**	words ending in **x**

Spelling problems can arise because children don't hear the second syllable in words such as **seven**. Have your child put his hand under his chin and feel how the jaw drops with each vowel sound: *sev·en.*

2. Say these words. How many vowels do you hear? How many do you see?

    upon   **seven**

Putting the Secret to Work

Word Families that end in *n*

1. Complete the word wheels. Say each rhyming word as you write it.

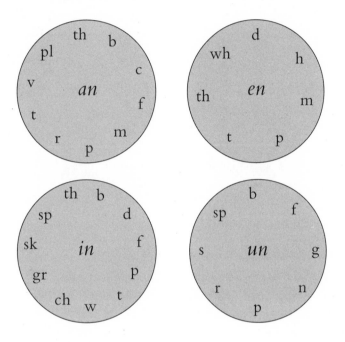

It's important to have your child say the pairs of words to hear which rhyme. Other pairs help him hear the difference in vowel sounds *(step-stop)* or consonant sounds *(lid—lip)*.

2. Say each pair of words carefully and write the rhyming pair in each list.

Dan—Sam	**can—con**	**chin—spin**
an—than	**bun—ban**	**den—them**
tan—tin	**when—then**	**sun—sin**

3. Read the sentence below. Can you make up a rule for when we use the word **a** and when we use **an**?

There is **an** apple, and **an** orange, and **a** banana.

We write the word **an** instead of **a** before a word that starts with a vowel. For example: **an apple, an egg, a carrot, a dog**.

Write **a** or **an** in front of these words.

__ bird	__ ostrich
__ animal	__ lion
__ insect	__ mosquito

Word Families that end in *p*

4. Complete the circles and triangles with words that end in **p**.

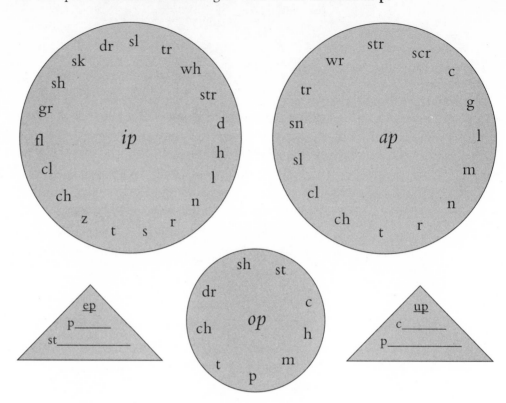

5. Completing sentences. Use the words from Exercise 4 to fill in the blanks in these sentences with words that rhyme.

The big *sh__ __* will *sl__ __* into the water.
The *tr__ __* will *sn__ __* and the mouse will be caught.
The police station is sometimes known as the *c__ __ sh__ __*.
The *ch__ __ d__ __* is delicious!
When you *sk__ __* with a rope, try not to *tr__ __*.

Word Families that end in *x*

6. Write the rhyming words ending in a short vowel plus **x**.

Fax is a new word in our language; it is a short form of **facsimile**.

ax: f__ __, M__ __, t__ __, w__ __
ex: s__ __, R__ __
ix: f__ __, m__ __, s__ __
ox: b__ __, f__ __
ux: t__ __ (short for tuxedo)

7. Fill in the **x** words that fit the meanings:
My friend __*ax* will __*ax* me about my income __*ax*.
Can you __*ix* my __*ux* by __*ix* o'clock?
The red __*ox* ate all the food in the __*ox*.

8. Unscramble and write the three Challenge Words.
n t a h   t e h n   e h n w

Write the two Challenge Words that are numbers. Circle the word that rhymes with **sun**.

— — —   — — — — —

9. Use the Challenge Words to complete this news flash!

> ## CALIFORNIA QUAKE!
> A huge earthquake, measuring almost __ __ *v* __ __ on the Richter Scale, has just hit California. It was much stronger __ *h* __ __ the quake three days ago. __*n*__ resident said he felt the shock *w*__ __ __ he was brushing his teeth. __ __ *e* __ another shock hit a few minutes later.

Home Connections

Word Wheels

Make rhyming words a game. Use two different-sized paper plates, joined together with a metal brad through their centres. Print the consonants on the smaller inner wheel and the rhyming endings on the larger wheel as shown. Have your child turn the outside wheel to each consonant and pronounce it, then write the word that can be made.

two paper plates

metal brad for centre

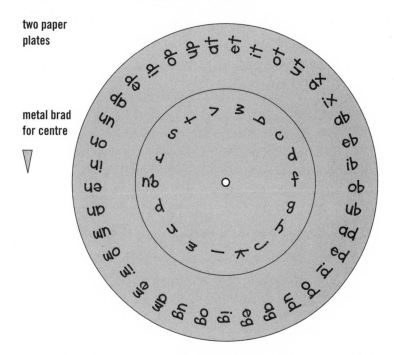

Reverse Dictation

To check letter recognition and pronunciation, give your child a list of short vowel words and have them dictate the words to you. (See Appendix II for word lists.)

In the Car

Watch for short vowel words on licence plates, where they often occur by accident.

Short Vowel and Consonant combinations: *ck*, *ch*, and *tch*; *st* and *sh*

Dictate the Unit and Challenge Words. Substitute your child's or a friend's name in the sentences whenever appropriate.

Unit Words

back	Ali was riding on the **back** of a horse.
last	He was the **last** one found in hide-and-seek.
truck	My dad drives a **truck**.
black	The robbers wore **black** from head to toe.
best	Her bike was the **best** present of all.
neck	Around her **neck** she was wearing diamonds.
just	There was **just** enough pop left for all of them.
much	There was so **much** noise they couldn't hear!
such	With **such** a selection, she couldn't choose.
wish	He closed his eyes and made a **wish.**
pitch	Can you **pitch** the ball with your left hand?
splash	The diver hit the water without a **splash.**
ask	Why don't you **ask** for the tickets?
cost	How much do those candies **cost**?
catch	He tried to **catch** the runaway hamster.

Challenge Words

which	**Which** one do you want?
scratch	Our dog likes to **scratch** behind his ears.
o'clock	They had to meet the messenger at six **o'clock**.
watch	He got a new **watch** for his birthday.
once	It happened all at **once**!

Rewrite any misspelled words. On the correctly spelled version, highlight the difficult part. For example:

dictation	rewrite
cash	ca<u>t</u>ch

What's the Secret?

Children can't hear the *t* in **catch**. They need to learn the words by shape as well as sound.

1. Say the words below. Which letter can't you hear? We call this a **silent letter.** Underline the silent letter in these words:

    pitch   catch   scratch   watch

2. Add **eck** to each letter below and write the words. Say them out loud. Notice that the vowel sound is still short.

    d __ __ __   **n** __ __ __   **ch** __ __ __

3. Add **est** and write the words. Say them out loud. Is the vowel sound still short?

   b __ __ __   **n** __ __ __   **r** __ __ __

Spelling Secret #5

Grouping words that end in consonant combinations such as **ch, ck, st,** and **sh** into rhyming families helps us spell them: **back—black; best—west.**

Putting the Secret to Work

1. Write the Unit and Challenge Words that fit these shapes. Circle the silent letter in each.

Word Families with *ch* and *tch*

2. Complete the word triangles below. Say each word and underline or circle the rhyming parts.

<u>atch</u>
b_____ c_____
m_____ scr_____ sn_____

<u>utch</u>
D_____ h_____
cl_____ cr_____

<u>otch</u>
n_____
bl_____ Sc_____

<u>itch</u>
h_____ d_____
p_____ gl_____
st_____ sw_____ tw_____

Write the three Unit and Challenge Words that end in **ch** but don't spell them with a **t:**

   *W*__ __ __ __ kid ate so *m*__ __ __ cake? I've never seen *s*__ __ __ a big eater!

3. Write the Challenge word that ends in **atch** but doesn't rhyme with **catch.**

   w __ __ __ __

   In many words beginning with **wa,** the vowel sound is similar to a short **o.** Say: **wash, water, want,** and **wand** and listen for the *o* sound as in **hot.**

Word Families with *ck*

4. Make as many words as you can from the word wheels. Say each word as you write it. Can you hear the rhyme?

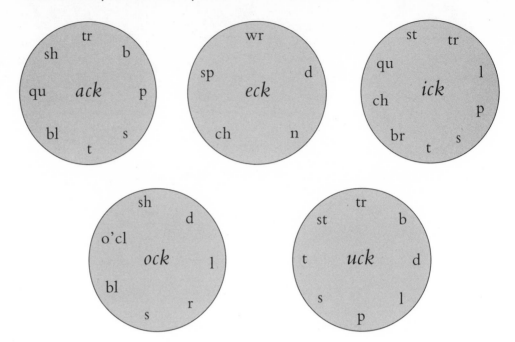

The Challenge Word **o'clock** comes from "of the clock." Over the centuries it was shortened to be o'clock.

Short words ending in the *k* sound almost always end in **ck**. The exceptions are brand names, like **Pac** Man, and Big **Mac**. (Longer two-syllable words, such as **comic** and **panic**, often end in **ic**.)

5. Which words rhyme? Write the rhyming pairs and circle or underline the rhyming parts.

neck—wreck	sock—suck	tick—tack	block—clock
deck—dock	tack—black	lick—pick	sack—sick

6. Write the Unit and Challenge Words that end with **ck** and fit the sentences.
   At four *o'cl*__ __ __ they drove their monster *tr*__ __ __ over the big *bl* __ __ __ rocks. Now the *b* __ __ __ __ of his *n* __ __ __ hurts!

Word Families with *st*

Awareness should be growing that although rhyming word families help us spell many short words in English, there are also exceptions. Help your child recognize that words such as **most** break the pattern. Contrast the vowel sound you hear in **most** with **cost** and **lost**.

7. Use the circles to make as many words ending in **st** as you can. Say each word as you write it and listen for the rhyme.

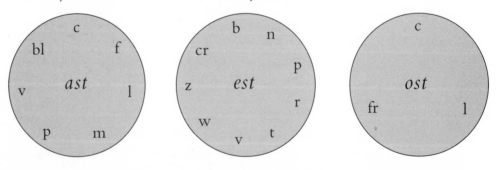

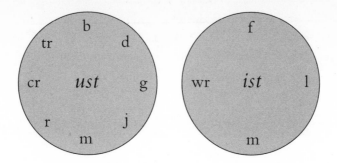

8. Write an ad! Use the Unit Words that end in **st** to complete this advertisement.

> ## SPECIAL SALE!
> Buy the *b* __ __ __ bike at the lowest *c* __ __ __ !
> This terrific mountain bike will *l* __ __ __ for years.

Word Families with *sh*

9. Write three words that rhyme with the words below.

wish	**d**_____	**f**_____
splash	**cr**_____	**d**_____
rush	**br**_____	**bl**_____

10. Unscramble and write these words that end in **sk**. Circle the one that is a Unit Word.

k s a   s e k d   k r s i   s k u d

11. The Challenge word **once** means one time. Your child can remember that it is spelled like **one** with a **c.** Finish this sentence:

Once upon a time...

Home Connections

The "Add-a-Consonant" Game

Many important Word Families end in two or more consonants (**back, catch, west**). It's fun to see how many consonants you can add to a short vowel, making new words each time. For example:

a
at
cat
catch
scratch

In all these words, the **a** keeps the short sound (as in *at*). Play a game in which you start with a single vowel: **a, e, i, o,** or **u.** Your child adds a consonant after the vowel to make a new word. Take turns making new words by adding consonants at the beginning or end. For example: **i, it, pit, pitch; a, at, fat, flat; e, end, bend, blend.** The person who makes the last word gets to choose the next letter.

It may be a good idea to begin a "tough word" list, to be tacked up on the fridge or a bulletin board. Your child can add words that are a special challenge, or just of particular interest. (For example, a list of difficult dinosaur names!) In this way vocabulary and spelling skills can be built at the same time.

UNIT 6

Word Families with Double Consonants

Dictate the Unit and Challenge Words, using the sentences provided, or your own.

Unit Words

off★	The apple rolled **off** the table.
all	She kept **all** her clothes in her closet.
with	He went to the store **with** his friends.
will	Pina said she **will** come over after school.
help	She wanted to **help** make the snow fort.
well	They looked deep down in the **well.**
boss	My mother's **boss** drives a red car.
call	Tony will **call** Sam on the car phone.
jump	He had to **jump** onto the truck.
fell	They **fell** off the swing in the park.
camp	Maria and Heather like to **camp** out in the back yard.
spell	She knows how to **spell** that word.
bath	Our dog needed a **bath** after he rolled in the mud.
class	There are twenty-eight people in my **class.**
staff	My teacher is the newest member of the **staff**.

★One of the 25 most frequently misspelled words

Challenge Words

if	What would you do **if** you had $1,000,000?
of	There was a bottle **of** syrup on the table.
until	Wait **until** the show is over to turn off the TV.
half	We can each have **half** of the doughnut.
saw	He couldn't believe what he **saw**!

Rewrite any misspellings and highlight the difficult parts.

What's the Secret?

1. Read the words below. What sound do you hear at the end? What do you notice about the final consonants?

all—ball—call   fell—spell—well

class—grass—mass   stiff—cliff—sniff

2. Say the pairs of words below. Write the pairs that rhyme.

cap—camp   limp—chimp

jump—pump   stop—stomp

If your child has difficulty spelling **camp** or **jump** she may have trouble hearing the **m**. Have her listen carefully to the difference between **cap** and **camp**.

Spelling Secret #6

Short words that end in **f**, **s**, and **l** usually double the final letter:

    call   **will**   **class**   **staff**

Grouping words that end in **mp** into rhyming families can help us spell them: **camp—stamp; jump—bump.**

    Doubling the final **f, s,** and **l** after short vowels is an important pattern in longer words such as **progress, sheriff,** and hundreds of words ending in **less** and **ness.**

Putting the Secret to Work

Word Families with *ll*

1. Write the rhyming words you can make in each balloon below.

Notice the difference between the sound of *a* in **bat** and **ball**. In **ball** it's more like a short *o*.

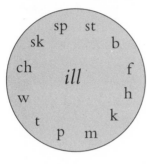 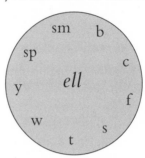 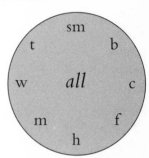

2. Which words rhyme? Say each pair in the lists below and write the words that rhyme.

The only common short o word with **oll** is **doll**.

bill—ball	**mill—mall**	**will—wall**	**gull—dull**
pill—bill	**mall—tall**	**sell—sill**	**dull—doll**
pill—ball	**fill—fell**	**sell—well**	**call—well**

3. Write the Unit Words that fit these sentences.

He can *sp__ __ __* really *w__ __ __*.

W__ __ __ you *c__ __ __* me to let me know?

She *f__ __ __* off her bike and hurt her knee.

Word Families with *ss*

4. Complete the triangles and wheels below. Say each rhyming word as you write it.

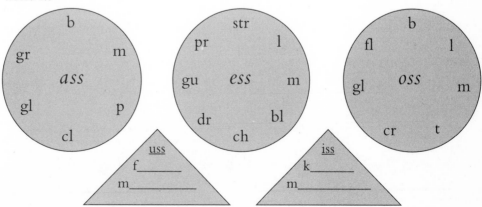

5. Unscramble the words that end in **ss** and fit the sentences.

He was a famous __ __ __ __ __ player at age twelve. **(h s e c s)**

Every night, I remember to __ __ __ __ __ my teeth. **(s l f o s)**

This tall __ __ __ __ __ has milk in it. **(a l s g s)**

Word Families with *ff*

6. Write the words that rhyme with **puff.**

c __ __ __, h __ __ __, st __ __ __, bl __ __ __,

fl __ __ __, gr __ __ __, scr __ __ __, sc__ __ __

7. The Challenge Words **of** and **if** break the double **f** rule. Use them in these sentences.

____ I were King ____ the Jungle, I'd be a lion.

____ I had a million dollars, I could buy the best ___ everything.

____ I were the strongest kid in the world, I wouldn't be afraid ____anyone!

8. The words **off** and **of** are often confused in spelling. Write the word that fits the meaning in the sentences below.

Get (**of, off**) my chair!

I took (**of, off**) my coat.

I'm afraid (**of, off**) dogs.

I want some (**of, off**) that cake.

There is a lot (**of, off**) money on the table.

Words with *lp* and *mp*

9. A few words end with **lp** like **help.** Write the words that fit the sentences.

I went on holiday to the *A__ps*.

The barber cut my hair so short you could see my *sc__ __p*.

When I saw the bear I yelled for *h __ __ p*.

The dog ate my ice cream in one big *g __ __ p*.

10. Write the Challenge Words that fit the clues.

I rhyme with **staff** and have a silent **l**: __ __ __ __

I have two syllables and end in **l**: __ __ __ __ __

You can cut with me and I rhyme with **paw**: __ __ __

As the big bad wolf says, "I'll **huff** and I'll **puff** and I'll blow your house down!"

11. Words ending in **short vowels** plus **mp** are more common than words that end in **lp**. Find the words listed in the margin in the Word Search:

s	t	a	m	p	m	i	l	a	g
p	m	a	r	l	f	j	p	l	y
h	k	s	w	u	c	x	m	z	n
b	s	t	o	m	p	m	o	h	c
s	p	u	m	p	m	a	r	q	d
l	e	m	r	b	a	d	h	p	l
u	s	p	v	f	h	u	a	t	a
m	p	m	a	c	c	m	v	m	m
p	m	i	h	c	q	p	w	c	p
t	d	l	g	p	m	u	j	s	k

damp   chomp
ramp   romp
lamp   dump
camp   pump
champ   lump
stamp   jump
limp   plump
chimp   stump
stomp   slump

Home Connections

Dictionary Skills: Alphabetical Order

Alphabetical order is so widely used in our lives that it is an important skill for children to practise.

Practise with personal phone books, looking up friends' names. Have your child start his or her own phone book (with tabs for letters of the alphabet if possible). Have your child find your name in the local telephone directory, and continue to practise which part of the book you will find it in—the beginning, middle, or end.

Indexes are also alphabetical. When you are cooking with your child, let him look up **cookies** or **salads**. Use the same tactic—where will you find cookies—in the beginning, middle, or end of the index?

UNIT 7

Dictate the Unit and Challenge Words. Repeat the words if your child doesn't hear them clearly.

Short Vowel and Consonant Combinations: *nd, ng, nt,* and *nk*

Unit Words

and	They collected rocks **and** shells at the beach.
went★	She **went** to Florida for her holiday.
thing	What is that **thing** in your hand?
long	Most girls in my class have **long** hair.
find	I can't **find** my dog.
think	It takes time to **think** of the answer.
told	Can you remember what he **told** you?
next	On the **next** page there is a hippopotamus.

thank	**Thank** you for the beautiful flowers.
left	The only flavour **left** is cherry.
want	What do you **want** for your birthday?
end	It was a good story from beginning to **end**.
slept	She **slept** until noon.
cent	He has only one **cent** left.
skunk	The **skunk** left a terrible smell behind.

Challenge Words

friend★	Carlo's **friend** Maria is 13 years old.
built	They **built** a doghouse for their dog.
talk	I love to **talk** on the phone.
second	We like to sit in the **second** row.
won	Look what I **won** at the party!

★One of the 25 most frequently misspelled words

In the words **think**, **thank**, and **thing**, the **th** is made by blowing out air without vibrating the vocal cords. Try **thin**, **than** to hear the difference.

Some people remember the **i** and **e** in friend by saying, "**I** am a **friend** to the **end**." Or they remember how to spell **build** from a sign on a lumber store: "**U** Build **It**."

Rewrite any misspelled words.

What's the Secret?

1. Which words rhyme? Say the pairs of words below and write the pairs that rhyme. Circle the rhyming parts.

thick—think   ring—thing   bent—went
pink—think   twig—thing   wet—went

2. Write the Challenge Words, filling in the blank letters. Circle the silent letters. Try to think of ways to remember the silent letters.

ta __ k   fr__ __ __ d   b __ __ lt

> ### Spelling Secret #7
> Grouping words in rhyming families with **n + consonants** helps spell many words: **and**, **sand**, **band**; **went**, **bent**, **tent**; **ring**, **thing**, **sing**.
> Smaller Word Families end in the consonant combinations **ld** or **ft**: **told**, **gold**, **old**; **left**, **heft**.

Putting the Secret to Work

Word Families with *nd, ng,* and *nt*

1. Complete the word eggs. Say each word as you write it.

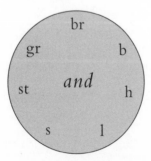
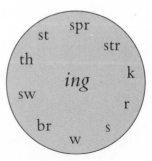

There are three words that sound the same but they all mean different things: **sent**, **scent**, and **cent**!

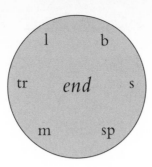

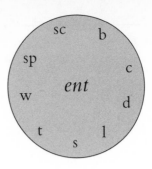

2. Write the Unit Words that fit these clues.

I rhyme with **song**, and mean the opposite of **short**. __ __ __ __

I rhyme with **kind**, and mean the opposite of **lose**. __ __ __ __

I have a short *o* sound spelled with **a,** and end with **t**. __ __ __ __

I rhyme with **bend** and mean the opposite of **begin**. __ __ __ __

I rhyme with **band** and mean something like **plus**. __ __ __

3. Write the three-letter Unit Words that fit this sentence.

I like the beginning __ __ __ the __ __ __ of that movie.

4. Many people confuse **went** and **want.** Write the correct word for these sentences.

He_____ to bed.

We _____ some ice cream.

She _____ to the store to get the bread.

Words starting with **ce** and **ci** are pronounced with an *s* sound. **Circle** and **city** are probably the two most important of these words. Notice the second **c** in circle sounds like *k*.

5. Listen to the sound at the beginning of the Unit Word **cent**. The letter **c** has two sounds, *s* and *k*. Listen to the sound of **c** in each word below and write it in the correct column. Can you find a pattern? (Hint—look at the second letters!)

cap, cent, city, cup, cell, car, cold, cut, centre, cat, circle

c sounds like s	c sounds like *k*
cent	cap

Word Families with *nk*

6. Complete the words in the word bubbles. As you write each word, say it out loud, and listen for the *nk* sound.

When children write **thak** instead of **thank**, they are actually closer to what we really hear! It takes practice with pairs such as set/sent, bed/bend, pick/pink to hear the **n plus consonant** at the end of words.

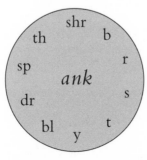

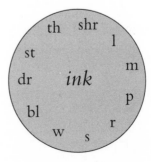

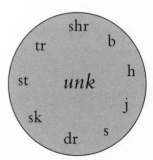

7. Write the pair of words that rhyme in each group below. Circle the rhyming parts.

bank—bunk	**lent—spent**	**bent—lend**
sink—sank	**hint—hunt**	**junk—sunk**
yank—blank	**bent—bunt**	**hung—long**

8. Write the Unit Words that fit this story.

I met a little *sk* __ __ __ last night.

He said, "I *th*__ __ __ you'd better leave."

Phew! I *l*__ __ __ as fast as I could.

Th __ __ __ you," said the *sk* __ __ __.

*N*__ __ __ time watch where you're going!

Word Families with *ld* and *ft*

9. Write three words that rhyme with **told.**

c __ __ __

s __ __ __

g __ __ __

10. Write words that:
- rhyme with **left**   th __ __ __
- rhyme with **lift**   g __ __ __, dr __ __ __, sh __ __ __

11. Write each Challenge Word, filling in the missing letters.

fr__ __nd   b__ __lt   t__ __k

sec__ __d   w__n

Write each word three more times, highlighting the difficult letters by:
- writing them in capitals: *fr* IE*nd*;
- writing them in different colours or highlighting them with a marker.

Home Connections

Dictionary Skills—Alphabetizing to the Second Letter.

Begin to practise putting words in alphabetical order by looking at the second letter in words. For example, in the cookbook index, ask your child which will come first? **cupcakes, cake, cookies**

In the class list, whose name will be first? **Jennifer, Jane, John**

In a mail-order catalogue, which item will come first? **sweaters, socks, sheets**

Give your child lists of three or four foods, clothing, names, and toys that begin with the same letter and have them put them in alphabetical order by looking at the **second** letter.

Look up the words **sent** and **scent** to check the meanings, or have fun looking for words ending in **ng** patterns. For example:

A famous video game	Donkey K_____
A famous city in China	H_____ K_____
A famous movie gorilla	K_____ K_____

Long Vowels

Long Vowels

Introduction

Beginning at grade two or somewhere between seven and ten years of age, many children are ready for the more complicated spelling patterns of long vowels. The long vowels say their own names: **a**, **e**, **i**, **o**, and **u**.

In order to learn long vowel patterns, children need to recognize that we can add a letter to a word to "make the sound long." Sometimes, the letter is an **e** at the end of the word. For example, look at what happens to the word **fat** when we add **e**. It becomes **fate**. In the same way:

hat becomes **hate**
bit becomes **bite**
hop becomes **hope**

Learning to spell the long vowel patterns must be solidly based on a child's experience with short vowels. Using a pattern marker such as a silent **e** is a much more abstract idea than knowing that a letter spells a sound. If you discover that your child has trouble hearing the difference between **hop** and **hope**, be sure to go back and work through some of the short vowel units again. Or perhaps your child has not reached this stage of development, and needs more experience reading and listening to stories and poems, and writing lists, notes, and his own stories.

Once the simple pattern of adding an **e** to make the vowel long is learned, we go on to learn to spell other long vowel patterns:

1. open patterns—a single vowel ending a word or syllable
   go, no, open   **be, me, even**
2. two vowels together
   tail, boat, bean   **say, key**

UNIT 8

Dictate the list. Be sure to give your child time to write each word.

Long Vowels *a* and *o*: *a*–Consonant–*e*, *o*–Consonant–*e*

Unit Words

home
came
made
name
hope
take
place
make

The fox has his **home** in the ground.
He **came** and knocked on the door.
Jamal **made** a bookmark for his mom.
Write your **name** at the top of the page.
I **hope** you have a good time.
Please **take** your turn.
They had no **place** to go.
Let's **make** apple pie for dessert.

hole	The bulldozer dug a big **hole** in the ground.
gave	Ellen **gave** away her old sweatshirt.
same	My coat is the **same** as yours.
woke	When she **woke** it was a sunny day.
those	Keep **those** bees away from me!
late	I hope he won't be **late** for the show.
chase	Even the cat joined in the **chase**.

Challenge Words

have	What do you **have** in your pocket?
come	Here **come** the elephants.
some	She held **some** candy in her hand.
done	After the dishes were **done** she went outside.
gone	She has **gone** to visit her grandparents.
love	You will **love** that movie!

Have your child rewrite any misspelled words, paying special attention to the final silent **e**.

The **e** makes the sound long. Although the final **e** in home is silent, its "job" is to make the **o** say its own name. Say **hop** and **hope** and make sure your child hears how the **o** changes.

What's the Secret?

1. Review the names of the vowels again **a, e, i, o, u**. The long vowels sound like the letter names. Say these words and listen for the long vowel sounds.

a in name
e in these
i in bike
o in home
u in cute

2. Say these pairs out loud. Listen for the short and long vowel sounds. Circle the vowel that is silent.

at—ate   hop—hope   mad—made   hat—hate

3. Say these pairs. Write the word with the long vowel sound.

mane—man   cod—code   gap—gape   note—not

Spelling Secret #8

When a vowel is long in a word, it says its own name. The silent **e** on the end of a word usually makes the vowel long: **came, home**.

Grouping words with **long a–consonant–e** and **long o–consonant–e** in rhyming families helps us spell them: **make, take, bake; hole, pole, role**.

Putting the Secret to Work

Rhyming families with *a*–consonant–*e*

1. Complete the word wheels, saying each word as you write it. Circle the vowels in each word.

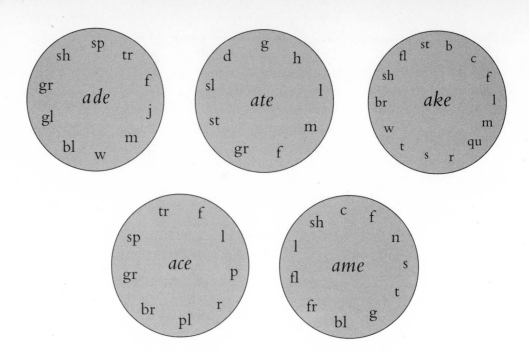

2. Write Unit Words and rhyming words to finish these sentences.

The princess g __ __ __ a little w __ __ __.

I'm glad you c __ __ __. What is your n __ __ __?

Open the g __ __ __ or I'll be l __ __ __ __!

In a big qu __ __ __ the earth will sh __ __ __.

The children r __ __ __ to find a pl __ __ __.

3. Write the Challenge Word that ends in **ave**. What sound does the **a** have—short *a* or long *a*? __ __ __ __

Word Families with *o*–Consonant–*e*

4. Complete the triangles below. Underline the vowels.

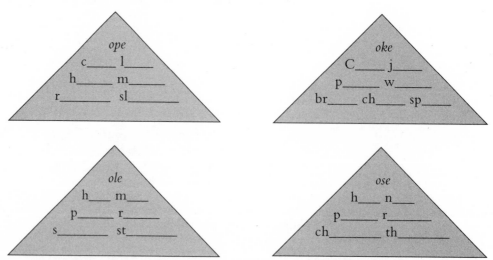

5. Write the Challenge Words that have the **o–consonant–e** pattern. Say them out loud and listen to the vowel sounds. Are they long or short?

c __ __ __   l __ __ __

g __ __ __   s __ __ __   d __ __ __

These important pronunciation exceptions to the pattern need to be memorized.

some (*sum*)
come (*cum*)
none (*nun*)
have (*hav*)
love (*luv*)
gone (*gon*)
give (*giv*)

Fortunately, words like **love** are used so often many children learn to spell them by sight.

6. Write the Unit Words that fit the clues.

I rhyme with **nose**. __ __ __ ⃝ __
I'm the place where you live. __ __ ⃝ __
An animal might live in me. __ ⃝ __ __
I rhyme with **poke** and you did it this morning. __ __ ⃝ __
I rhyme with **rope**, and you need me. __ __ __ ⃝

Write the circled letters to make a word with a long **o** that is something you should never do! __ __ __ __ __

7. Make new words by adding **e**. See how it changes the vowel sounds. Say the two words together and listen for the changes in sound.

mat__	man__	rob__	fat__
can__	rod__	fad__	cap__
gap__	tap__	not__	glob__

Home Connections

Have your child listen for vowel sounds in rhyming words (**came—name**). Continue to read lots of rhyming poems and picture books.

Older children can look in magazines, newspapers, and books for the **vowel–consonant–e** pattern. Your child may notice that there are other ways to spell long vowels. Don't worry, we will get to those!

Dictionary Skills

Phonetic marks. Have your child look up some of the words you made in the word wheels or triangles. For example: **gape** and **glade**. Remind them to look at the second letter, if both words begin with **g.**

Notice how the word is written in brackets with no **e** and a line over the **a.** The line tells us that the sound is long—pronounced like the letter name: (**gāp**), (**glād**).

UNIT 9

Word Families with long *i*: *i*–Consonant–*e*

Dictate the Unit and Challenge Words to your child. Leave space to the right for your child to rewrite misspelled words, or use the form on page 159 .

Unit Words

like	I **like** the summer holidays.
time	She looked at the clock to see the **time**.
nice	He is a **nice** boy.
five	There were **five** students away today.
white	We looked out at the sparkling **white** snow.
live	The **live** animals were kept in cages.
while	What happened **while** I was gone?

ride	They went for a **ride** on the horse.
life	**Life** without colds would be great!
prize	First **prize** is a trip to Italy.
bike	She rode her **bike** the whole way.
kite	The **kite** flew as high as the clouds.
nine	**Nine** out of ten people like that TV show.
pipe	Water rushed out of the burst **pipe**.
wise	An owl is supposed to be **wise**.

Challenge Words

awhile	You'll have to wait **awhile** for that dessert.
write	Don't forget to **write** lots of letters.
complete	I have the **complete** set of comic books.
these	I'd like some of **these** nice flowers, please.
sometimes	The baby **sometimes** cries when she's hungry.

Have your child underline or circle difficult parts as she rewrites misspelled words.

dictation	rewrite	posttest
wile	while	
pris	prize	

What's the Secret?

1. Say these words. Write the words with a long **i** or long **e**.

    ride   **bit**   **these**   **rip**

2. Add **e** to **bit** and **rip** and write the words. Say them out loud. How has the vowel sound changed?

    bit__   **rip__**

Spelling Secret #9

Many words with the sound of long *i* are spelled with the **i–consonant–e** pattern. The **e** makes the sound of the **i** long: **bike, kite, pipe, white**. Very few short words with the sound of long *e* follow the **e–consonant–e** pattern. Important exceptions are: **these, scene, theme, scheme**. Some two-syllable words end in **e–consonant–e**. For example: **complete, Chinese, extreme**.

Putting the Secret to Work

1. Say the words and write the rhyming pairs.

    bit—bite   **nice—slice**   **spin—nine**

    ride—side   **rip—pipe**   **smile—while**

Large Word Families with *i*–Consonant–*e*

2. Complete the word tires with rhyming words that end in **i–consonant–e**.

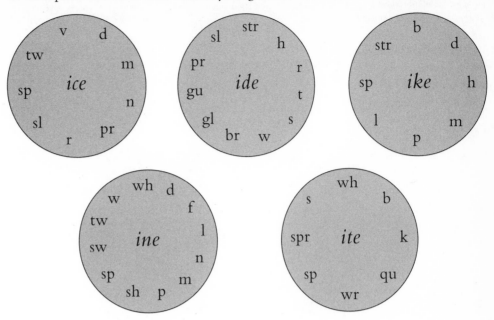

One way for children to remember the silent letters in words is to concentrate on how the word looks. Have them write the word with a different colour for the silent letters. Other words with silent *w* are: **wrong, wrist, wrinkle,** and **wrap**.

3. Unscramble the Unit and Challenge words that fit the sentences. Write the words and say them out loud, listening for the long *i* sound.

When you were **e i n e** you could **d r i e** a **k e i b.**

I'd **e l i k** to give you this **c e n i   h w t i e   t e k i.**

Unscramble the Challenge Word with a silent *w*.

I will **r t w i e** a letter to my friend.

Smaller Word Families with *i*–Consonant–*e*

4. Complete the word triangles with rhyming words that end in **i–consonant–e**.

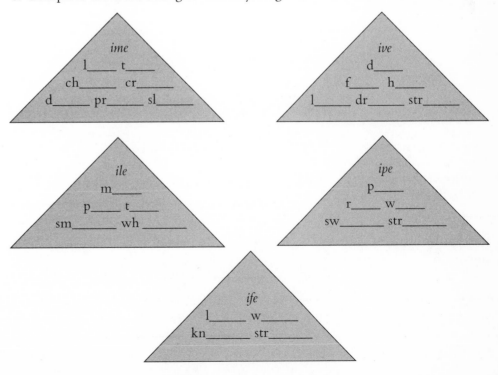

Give and the rhyming word **live** are exceptions to the **long vowel–consonant–silent e** pattern. But the words are written so often children usually learn them by sight. You can help by pointing out that no words in English end in **v**, except abbreviations such as **rev** for **revolution**.

5. Write the Unit Word that rhymes with **five** and fits this sentence.

We heard a __ __ __ __ recording of the concert.

Live can also be pronounced to rhyme with **give** (and has a different meaning), as in "I **live** in the city."

6. Dictionary Skills. Write these words in alphabetical order:

five   _____

life   _____

while   _____

awhile   _____

pipe   _____

time   _____

7. Write the Challenge Words that have these shapes.

Write the two Challenge Words that are made up of two small words. Circle each of the smaller words.

— — — — — — — —

— — — — — —

Home Connections

Writing words such as **write**, **prize**, and **awhile** four or five times can help fix the visual pattern in a child's mind. Most people have scribbled a word they weren't sure of on a scrap of paper, to see which spelling "looks right."

If you have a home computer, typewriter or any keyboard, children can practise "typing" the words. Looking for the letters helps the child focus on individual letters and their sequence in a word. As they become more expert on a keyboard the mechanical repetition helps fix the order of the letters in the child's mind. Otherwise, have your child manipulate magnetic letters, Scrabble ® tiles, or alphabet cards you make yourself. Scramble the letters of words and have your child sort them out.

UNIT 10

Long *e* as in *bee*: *e*, *ee*, *ea*, and *y*

Say each word, read the sentence, and say the word again. Ask your child to write them in a list like the one below.

Unit Words

me	Wait for **me** at the corner.
be	What can this **be** in the parcel?
three	There are **three** more days until my birthday.
she	How is **she** feeling?
see	Lara could **see** a boat on the lake.
many	How **many** people are waiting?

we	Here **we** go again!
tree	Up in the **tree** there is a nest.
eat	What would you like to **eat** for lunch?
even	There is an **even** number of chairs.
he	I'd say **he** is a very good dancer.
been	She has **been** all over the world.
teach	Can you **teach** me a card trick?
key	Have you got a **key** to the house?
pretty	That's a very **pretty** picture of your aunt.

Challenge Words

really	That is a **really** big piece of cake!
every	We see the old man **every** day.
behind	I found my book **behind** the couch.
began	The story **began** with "Once upon a time."
radio	She turned on the **radio** to hear the weather.

Go over the words your child has written. Point out what is right, as well as mistakes. For example, if your child spells **pretty** as **prety**, tell her she has five out of six letters right! Now she just needs to focus on writing two **t**'s instead of one.

These words have two syllables and two vowel sounds.

Rewrite any misspelled words.

What's the Secret?

1. Write the words below. Which vowel sound do you hear in each one? Underline the letters that spell that sound.

> **she   tree   eat**

2. Say each word. How many vowel sounds do you hear? Underline the letter or letters that spell a long **e** sound as in **bee**.

> **pretty   behind   many**

Spelling Secret #10

There are many ways to spell long *e* as in **bee**. Some of the most common ways are: **e** (he, she), **ee** (week), **ea** (eat), **y** (many).

To spell these words, we have to remember how they look as well as how they sound.

Putting the Secret to Work

Words with long *e* spelled *e*

1. Match the Unit Words that end with **e** with the sentences. Say each word. Listen for the long *e* as in **bee.**

Will you __ __ my friend?	**me**
__ __ __ is a happy person.	**be**
__ __ is a funny boy.	**we**
__ __ are two lucky people.	**she**
It's mine. Give it to __ __!	**he**

Notice that the **k** in **knee** and **kneel** is silent.

Word Families with long *e* spelled *ee*

2. Fill in the word triangle with words that rhyme and end in **ee.**

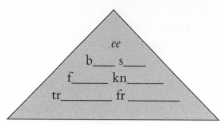

ee
b___ s___
f_____ kn_____
tr_____ fr_____

3. Write two Unit Words to finish these lines of poetry by Joyce Kilmer.
I think that I shall never __ __ __
A poem lovely as a __ __ __ __.

4. Complete the word balloons and say each rhyming word as you write it.

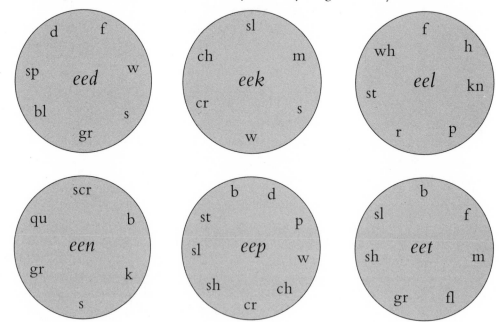

eed d f w s gr bl sp

eek sl ch m cr s w

eel f h kn p r st wh

een scr qu b k s gr

eep b d p w ch cr sh sl st

eet b f m fl gr sh sl

Been is a tricky word because it is sometimes pronounced *bin.*

Word Families with long *e* spelled *ea*

5. An old spelling rule says: "When two vowels go walking, the first one does the talking." Which vowel comes first in **eat**? Which vowel sound do you hear—*e* or *a*? Not all words follow the rule, but it is still useful.
Complete the word ovals. Say each word. Do you hear the long *e* sound?

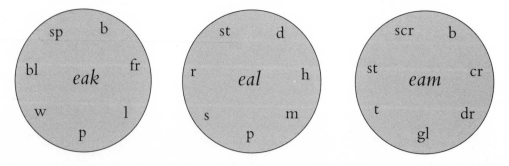

eak sp b fr l p w bl

eal st d h m p s r

eam scr b cr dr gl t st

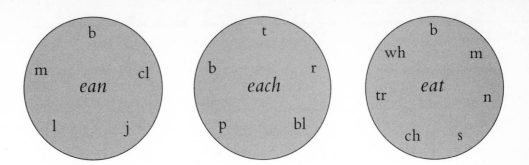

We call words that sound the same but mean something different **homonyms**. More about them in Unit 31.

6. Sometimes two words sound the same (**meet, meat**) but they are two different words with two different meanings. Match the words below with the right sentence.

week/weak
After his fall, he was too __ __ __ __ to move.
There are seven days in a __ __ __ __.
be/bee
The __ __ __ stung my foot.
I will __ __ home before five.
meat/meet
Can you __ __ __ __ me at the store?
I want to buy some __ __ __ __ for dinner.

7. Unscramble the Unit Words to finish this sentence.
I want you to **e h c t a** me to **t a e** with chopsticks.

Words with long *e* spelled *y*

8. Many words end with a **y** that sounds like the long **e** as in **bee**. Find the words for each letter of the alphabet (except **g, y,** and **x**) in the puzzle that end in **y.** Give yourself a point for each one you find.

Word searches are good because they help children focus on the order or sequence of the letters in words.

any	**many**	b	y	p	p	a	h	d	c	d	v
baby	**pretty**	s	i	l	l	y	e	i	y	f	e
crazy	**queasy**	e	g	i	t	j	f	z	n	h	r
dizzy	**really**	l	v	t	k	b	a	z	a	n	y
every	**silly**	m	i	e	m	a	n	y	y	r	h
fancy	**tidy**	k	t	n	r	b	c	s	t	e	t
happy	**ugly**	c	r	a	z	y	y	a	t	a	l
ivy	**very**	y	l	l	e	j	o	e	e	l	a
jelly	**wealthy**	t	i	d	y	l	g	u	r	l	e
kitty	**zany**	i	v	y	d	a	l	q	p	y	w
lady										

What's a key that climbs a tree? A monkey!

9. A small but useful group of words end in **ey: monkey, turkey, hockey, jockey, money.** Write the Unit Word that spells long **e** with **ey.** k__ __

Words such as **radio** end in the sound *eo*, spelled **io**. **Patio**, **studio**, **audio** are some examples. Also, many Italian boys' names such as **Antonio**, **Mario**, and **Fabrizio** end with **io**.

10. Write the Challenge Words that fit the clues:

I have <u>two</u> long **e** sounds: __ **ea**__ __ **y**

We both <u>begin</u> with **be**: **be**__ __ __ __, **be**__ __ __

I have a long **e** sound spelled with **i**: __ __ __ **i**__

I have three vowels, but you only hear two: **e**__**e**__**y**

Home Connections

Many names end in **y**. Have your child think of children in his class, friends, or relatives, and write the names that end in the long *e* sound, spelled **y.** Some popular names: Cindy, Tony, Cathy, Danny, Nicky, Jenny.

Help make writing a part of your child's daily life. Encourage your child to write notes, greeting cards, telephone messages, shopping lists and stories. Leave notes for your children on a family bulletin board, the fridge or their pillows. Invite them to write back to you.

Dictionary Skills: Look up words with long **i** and long **e** in the dictionary (such as **bike** and **be**). Notice the spelling in brackets after the word. The "hat" over the **i** and **e** tells you the sound is long (**bīk, bē**).

UNIT 11

Long *a: ay* and *ai*

Dictate the Unit and Challenge Words. If a word has two syllables, such as **again**, say it clearly, but naturally.

Unit Words

way	Which **way** did the robbers go?
again★	Once **again** she called out to him.
play	Katia had been waiting to **play** cards for a long time.
away	The bird flew **away** from the window.
afraid	Marco was **afraid** to go into the empty house.
say	Just **say** what's on your mind.
wait	Hey, guys, **wait** for me!
day	It was a beautiful **day**.
brain	Most dinosaurs had a very small **brain**.
maybe	**Maybe** it will rain today.
stay	She decided to **stay** home.
paint	Ricka and her friends are going to **paint** her room.
always	He **always** forgets to put the cap on the toothpaste.
tail	The baby pulled the dog's **tail.**
okay	It's **okay** with me.

Challenge Words

they★
great
break
steak
straight

★One of the 25 most frequently misspelled words.

Check the word list with your child. Notice how he is spelling the long a sound in words such as rain.

Where did **they** go?
That was **great** chocolate ice cream!
Try to **break** the record in your race today.
I would like my **steak** medium rare, please.
Linda's hair is very **straight**.

What's the Secret?

1. Say these words. Which vowel sound do you hear?

   way   say   day   stay

Write the words and underline the letters that make the long *a* sound.

2. Write these words and underline the two vowels in each one. Do these words follow the pattern "When two vowels go walking, the first one does the talking"?

   wait   brain   paint   tail

3. The words below are divided into syllables. Say the words and listen for the syllable that we say a bit louder and with more force than the other. We call this the *stressed* syllable.

   may•be   al•ways   a•fraid   a•gain

Write the words and underline the *stressed* syllable.

Spelling Secret #11

The long *a* sound can be spelled **ay** as in **day**. We usually find this spelling at the end of words: **away, day, say**.

When the two vowels **a** and **i** go walking in a word, the **a** does the talking: **aim, wait, brain, tail**.

Putting the Secret to Work

Word Families with *ay*

Notice that the word **says** (as in: He **says** his name is Bill) is pronounced like *ses*, but spelled like **say + s**.

1. Fill in the word poles with words that end in **ay.**

b⃝ __ __   p⃝l __ __
d __ __   l⃝ __ __
r⃝ __ __   j __ __
w __ __   st __ __
c⃝l __ __   t⃝r __ __
h __ __   s __ __
m __ __   g⃝r __ __
p __ __   s⃝tr __ __

Use the circled letters to fill in the answer to this riddle.

Student: What does B.C. stand for?

Teacher: __efo__e   __ a __cu__a__o__ __.

2. Unscramble the Unit Words that fit these sentences.

y w a a   t y s a   s w a l a y   y k o a   e y b m a

Sleepover

I want my best friend to __ __ __ __ overnight.

My mom __ __ __ __ __ __ says __ __ __ __ __.

I hope Mom will say __ __ __ __ tonight.

I don't want her to go __ __ __ __. We're having too much fun!

3. Write nine longer words that also end in **ay.**

birth__ __ __

Sun__ __ __

Mon__ __ __

Tues__ __ __

Wednes__ __ __

Thurs__ __ __

Fri__ __ __

Satur__ __ __

holi__ __ __

The days of the week are always written with a capital letter, as are the names of people and countries. We call them proper nouns.

Holiday was once two words, **holy** and **day**, as most holidays were religious celebrations.

Word Families with *ai*

4. Complete the word wheels and triangle to make words with long *a* sound spelled **ai.** Say each word as you write it and underline the vowels.

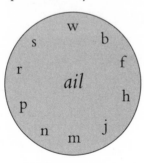

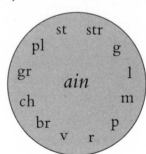

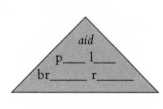

5. Write the Unit and Challenge Words with **ai** that fit the clues.

afraid again wait brain paint tail straight

clue								
not curved				a	i			
scared				a	i		▓	▓
once more	▓			a	i		▓	▓
inside your head	▓			a	i		▓	▓
don't go	▓	▓		a	i		▓	▓
put it on with a brush	▓	▓		a	i			▓
the end of an animal	▓	▓		a	i		▓	▓

6. Again is often spelled incorrectly, because we say it quickly and the vowel sounds like a short *e* or *i* (*agen* or *agin*). Write the word, underlining the letters that are hard to spell.

ag__ __n

They is one of the twenty-five most commonly misspelled words. Many children spell it with an **a** to match the sound.

It may help your child to know there are almost no words with a long *a* spelled **ae**. **Sundae** and **reggae** are two that do.

7. Write the Challenge Word that rhymes with **play** but ends in **ey** instead of **ay**: __ __ __ __ __

Write the Challenge Word that has six consonants, two of them silent!

__ __ __ __ __ __ __ __

8. Write the Challenge Words with the long *a* sound spelled *ea*. Do these words follow the "two vowels go walking" pattern?

gr __ __ t   st __ __ k   br__ __k

Home Connections

Keep building the idea of spelling patterns in your child's mind. Song lyrics like "The **rain** in **Spain** falls **main**ly in the **plain**" are built on words that sound alike and are spelled the same way.

Continue to read rhyming stories and poems to your child, and to teach them easy rhymes to recite. It sounds like a simple idea, but this is how the sound and spelling patterns of our language get fixed in our heads. For example, when it is raining outside, this is a good old rhyme to say:

Rain, **rain**, go **away**
Come **again** another **day**
Little Kelly wants to **play**.

Dictate the list of words with long **i**. The sentences make the meaning clear. They will help your child spell words that sound the same such as **by** and **buy**.

Long *i*: *i*, *y*, and *igh*

Unit Words

I	Start when **I** say go!
my	Would you like to come to **my** party?
by	The bird flew right **by** the window.
night	It was a dark and stormy **night**.
why	She wondered **why** it had happened.
might	Josh's cousins **might** come to visit.
high	The kite was so **high** you could hardly see it.
sky	The **sky** was clear of clouds today.
pie	Mark stuck his finger in the lemon **pie**.
try	I will **try** to catch up.
fight	Our dog got into a terrible **fight**.
reply	They waited ten days for a **reply**.
myself	I can make pancakes all by **myself**.
tiger	The **tiger** lives in India.
right	That's the **right** answer.

Challenge Words

sign	At the stop **sign**, turn left.
buys	When she goes shopping, she always **buys** some cookies.
goodbye	The children waved **goodbye** to their grandparents.
eye	My cat has one green **eye**, and one blue.
island	The country Iceland is an **island**.

Rewrite any misspelled words. Circle or underline the difficult letters on the recopied version.

dictation	rewrite
sine	sign

What's the Secret?

1. Sort these words into columns according to the way they spell the long *i*.
might, tiger, why, my, fight, sign, high, sky, island, myself

i	igh	y

2. Notice the position of **y** and **igh** in the words on your chart. Is it likely that the word **item** could be spelled **ightem** or **ytem**? Why not?

Spelling Secret #12

The letter **i** often spells long *i* at the beginning of words: **island**, **item**, **Irish**. The letter **y** often spells long *i* at the end of words: **try**, **my**, **why**. The letters **igh** spell long *i* at the end of a word or before **t**: **high**, **might**, **night**.

Putting the Secret to Work

Rhyming Words with *y*

1. Make as many words as you can from the circle.

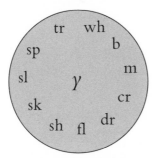

2. Use the Unit Words that end in **y** in the letter below.

try, sky, reply, why, by, my

```
August 5
To the Ideal Picture Co.

Dear Sirs,
I'm writing to ask __ __ __ you have not filled __ __order,
which I sent in on July 4th. I ordered a painting
called "Red __ __ __ at Sunset." Please __ __ __ to let me
know __ __ Thursday if you can send it to me. I will wait
for your __ __ __ __ __!

Your unhappy customer,
Ravi Shikar
```

3. Write the Unit Word that is made up of two smaller words.

m __ __ __ __ f

Rhyming Words that end in *ight*

4. Make as many words as you can from the circle. This is a large and important word family.

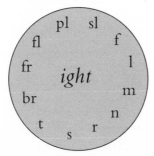

5. Write a four-letter Unit Word that rhymes with **sigh**: __ __ __ __

6. Write the Unit Words that fit these clues. Which word did you use twice?

opposite of day   __ __ __ __ (○)

opposite of wrong   __ __ __ (○) __

a violent struggle   __ (○) __ __ __

possibility **or** strength   __ __ (○) __ __

opposite of left   __ __ __ (○) __

Use the circled letters to write a word that rhymes with **high** and means part of your body. __ __ __ __ __.

7. Write the small family of words that rhymes with **pie** and spells long *i* with **ie**.

```
     p____ | t____
     l____ | d____
```

8. Unscramble the words with long *i* spelled *i* that fit the clues. One is a Unit Word. One is a Challenge Word.

a large fierce striped animal	e t r i g
people who come from Ireland	s r i h I
a piece of land surrounded by water	n i d l s a
a word that means very, very small	i y t n
a green climbing plant	v y i

It's not easy to remember the **g** in **sign**.
The word **sign** comes from the word **signal**. Say the two words out loud. What has happened to the *g* sound in signal?

9. These five Challenge Words all have long *i*. Write them and underline parts that are hard to remember.

sign   **buys**   **goodbye**   **eye**   **island**

10. Write the Challenge Words that fit these shapes.
Shape boxes are useful to help us remember difficult words.

11. Two Challenge Words spell long *i* with **ye**. Use them to complete this rhyme.

If you throw that p**ie**

In my __ __ __

I'm saying good__ __ __!

12. There are three ways to spell **bi**.

    by   buy   bye

You have to think about the meaning of the sentence to know which word to use. Write the correct word for each of these sentences.

Please be here __ __ six o'clock.

I want to __ __ __ a new bike.

He's going home __ __ train.

He said "__ __ __" and ran out the door.

Eggs are sold __ __ the dozen.

Home Connections

The **ight** spelling in **night** and **light** may be slowly changing to **ite** in North America. You and your child will notice words like **lite** on many products and signs. You might also find **brite** for **bright** and **rite** for **right**. (**Rite** is a real word—it means a ceremony or custom as in "the **rites** of spring.")

In the meantime **ight** is still the correct spelling. Your child can practise with this old wishing rhyme:

Star *l*__ __ __ __

Star *br*__ __ __ __

First star I see *ton*__ __ __ __

Wish I may, wish I *m*__ __ __ __

Have the wish I wish *ton*__ __ __ __.

UNIT 13

Long *o*: *o*, oa, and *ow*

Unit Words

oh	"**Oh**, no!" she called out, as she sped down the hill.
go	You **go** first, I'm afraid of that sled.
old	How **old** are you?
over	Put the presents **over** there on the table.
boat	Sam's **boat** zoomed over the water.
only	I have **only** three friends who are my age.
so	It is **so** nice to see you!
throw	Try to **throw** the ball to the catcher.
road	They live on a very busy **road**.
ago	A long time **ago**, buffalo roamed the prairies.
also	I **also** have a brother named Chris.
own	How many coats do you **own**?
hello	Say **hello** to my friend.
no	My dad said **no** more cookies!
open	Please **open** this jar of pickles.

Challenge Words

know★
almost
though
goes
ocean

★One of the 25 most frequently misspelled words.

Check the list with your child.

Writing simple words in syllables helps children practise breaking words into smaller parts for spelling and pronunciation.

In words with **ow**, the **w** acts like a vowel the way **y** does in words such as **day**.

The letters **ow** are a tricky pattern because they some-times say **ow!** as in **how**. Watch out for this pair: He had a **bow** and arrow. She took a **bow** after her recital.

How do you **know** that is true?
Jan is **almost** twelve years old.
Even **though** she is blind, she goes everywhere.
Lisa **goes** to my school.
The ship sailed across the **ocean.**

Rewrite any words you spelled incorrectly, paying special attention to the spelling of long *o*.

What's the Secret?

1. Say these words out loud. What vowel sound do you hear? Do these words follow the rule "When two vowels go walking, the first one does the talking?"

boat   **road**   **float**

2. Say these words out loud. Which letter spells long *o*?

go   **so**   **no**   **old**

In these two-syllable words, which letter spells long *o*? Write the words with a space between syllables. Underline the syllable we say with more force or stress.

o•pen   **o•ver**   **on•ly**   **al•so**   **hell•o**   **a•go**

3. Say these words out loud. Which two letters spell the long *o* sound?

throw   **own**   **show**   **know**

Spelling Secret #13

The long *o* sound can be spelled **o** as in **go**, **open**, **old**.
When the two vowels **oa** go walking, the **o** does the talking as in: **boat**, **road**, **goal**. Some words spell long *o* with **ow**: **own**, **throw**, **know**.

Putting the Secret to Work

Rhyming families with *o, oa,* and *ow*

1. Write the rhyming words that fit these patterns:

o
s____
g____ n____
oat
c____
g____ m____
bl_____ fl____ thr____
ow
b____ l____
r____ t____ m____
bl____ gl____ gr____
cr____ sh____ sl____ sn____
st____ thr____ kn____ fl____

2. Write the Unit Words with long *o* that fit the story your grandfather might tell.

> Long **a__ __** we had a **b__ __ __**. The lake was **o__ __ __** a short way down the **r __ __ __**. It was **s__** much fun to **g__** and **o__ __ __** the boathouse and row our **b__ __ __ o__ __ __** to our friend's dock. They **a__ __ __** had a boat. "**He__ __ __**," we would call, then we would **th__ __ __** a rope for them to catch. **__h**, I think there was **n__** more fun in the world than fishing from that **o__ __** boat on a summer's day.

Rhyming words with *oa*

3. Write rhyming words for each.

> **road** t_____ l_____
>
> **boat** g_____ fl_____ c____

If your child is unfamiliar with the word **verb**, say it is an action word such as **swim** or **run** that tells what we are doing.

4. The Challenge Word **goes** is part of the verb **to go**. All the words below are related to this verb. Match the correct word to these sentences.

> We are _____ to school. **went**
>
> My dad has _____ to work. **going**
>
> She _____ to work every day. **go**
>
> They _____ to the movies yesterday. **gone**
>
> My friend can _____ with me. **goes**

5. Unscramble the Challenge Words that fit this puzzle.

> **w k o n   m s t o l a   g h t h o u   s o g e   c n a e o**
>
> Alisa ◯__ __ __ to a special school.
>
> The hot chocolate was __ ◯__ __ __ __ too hot to drink!
>
> We __ __ __ __ __ a lot of people at that school.
>
> Even __ __ __ ◯__ __ it was cold, we had fun.
>
> There is a lot of salt in the __ __ ◯__ __!

Use the circled letters to answer this riddle.

> **What stick doesn't grow on a tree?**
>
> **A __ __ __ __ stick!**

6. The Challenge Word **though** has three silent letters: **ugh**. Have your child say the word and write it three times. Each time, use a different colour for the silent letters.

No and **know** are two different words that sound the same. **No** means not so, while **know** means having knowledge.

7. Many children (and adults too!) make mistakes with **no** and **know**. Practise using the correct word in these sentences.

> __ __ more candy for you!
>
> I __ __ __ __ the answer.
>
> __ __ __ __ when to say __ __!
>
> There's __ __ way to fix it that I __ __ __ __ of.

Your child can remember **ocean** by saying it means sea and there's a c in the word.

8. Write the two Challenge Words with two syllables.

> ____•_____   ____•_____

Write the Challenge Word that spells **sh** with **c**.

> _____

Home Connections

Dictionary Skills: How can your child look up **know**, if she doesn't **know** it begins with a silent **k**? A good dictionary, such as the *Gage Junior Dictionary*, will list it under **no**.

> ☞ Homonyms. **No** is pronounced like **know**.

Now she can look up **know** and check the meaning.
In the same way, if your child looks up **by**, she will find **bye** and **buy**.

> ☞ Homonyms. **By** is pronounced like **buy** and **bye**.

Teach your child an old song with long *o*:
    Row, row, row your boat.
    Gently down the stream.
    Merrily, merrily, merrily, merrily
    Life is but a dream.

UNIT 14

Long *u*: *o, oo, ew*, and *ue*

Dictate the Word List. Use sentences to help make the meaning of words such as **to**, **too**, and **two** clear.

Unit Words

to	Chin went **to** the store with his brother.
do	What **do** you want for breakfast?
you	**You** have very nice eyes.
too	That costs **too** much money!
new	Brad has a **new** skateboard.
blue	My favourite colour is **blue**.
soon	It will **soon** be summer.
two	She has **two** sisters.
few	There are a **few** cookies left.
shoot	Don't **shoot** that water pistol at me!
room	My **room** is painted white.
use	Please **use** your own toothbrush!
cute	That's a **cute** kitten.
huge	The dinosaur was **huge**.
glue	The **glue** didn't stick very well.

Challenge Words

knew	Jan **knew** the pot was too hot to touch.
suit	He has to wear a **suit** to the wedding.
fruit	My favourite **fruit** is peaches.
who	Do you know **who** has the ball?
into★	She put the pill **into** her mouth.

Check the list. If your child made errors with **to**, **two**, and **too** tell her that this unit will help her learn when to use each one.

The letter **w** acts as a vowel in words such as **new** and **few**.

Rewrite any misspelled words.

What's the Secret?

1. Say these words out loud. Write each word and circle the letters that make the long *u* sound as in **you**.

blue   soon   too

2. Say these words. How is the long **u** sound different than in the words above?

few   cute   huge

> ### Spelling Secret #14
>
> The long *u* sound is pronounced **yu**, as in y**ou** and sometimes **oo** as in s**oo**n. We spell long *u* in different ways: **u–consonant–e** (huge, cute); **ew** (ew, new); **oo** (soon, room, too).
>
> Smaller groups of words spell long *u* with these patterns: **ue** (blue, glue); **ui** (fruit, suit); **o** (do, who).

Putting the Secret to Work

1. Three of the Unit Words sound the same. Match the meaning and spelling below.

to   also, more than enough

too   one more than one

two   in the direction of

Write the word **to**, **too**, or **two** that fits the meaning of the sentences below.

The _____ boys are brothers. They are going _____ the baseball game at _____ o'clock. It's _____ far _____ walk, so they will have _____ take _____ buses _____ the ball park.

Word Families with *oo*

2. Write the rhyming words to complete each circle. Say the words as you write them and listen for the long *u*.

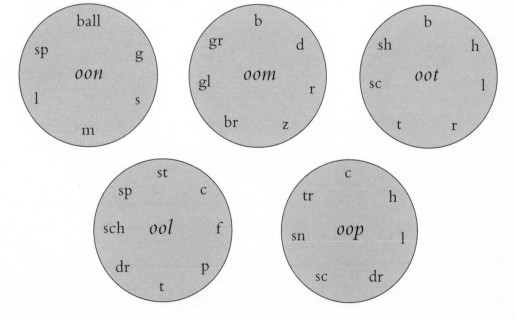

The word **wool** is an exception to the **ool** pattern. The letters **oo** have the same sound as in **book**.

Words with *u*-consonant-*e*

3. Write words that end in **u-e** combinations.

ute	fl____	br____	c____
use	f____	m____	am_____
ude	d____	n____	r____
uge	h____	ref_____	
ule	r____	m____	y_____

4. Write the Unit Words that end in **ute** and **uge** to finish this sentence:

That *h*__ __ __ monster has a *c*__ __ __ face!

The *ew* family

Do you pronounce **new** as *nyu* or *noo*? Both pronunciations are correct. The same is true of **dew**.

5. Complete the circle. Say each word as you write it. Notice whether the long **u** has a *yu* or *oo* sound.

6. Use **new** and **knew** in the sentences below:

I _____ you were going to call me.

Our _____ phone is really neat.

7. Use these Unit Words to complete this ad.

new, too, use, do, few, you, soon, blue, to

*D*__ *y*__ __ want the whitest, brightest clothes? *N*__ __ *b*__ __ __ Super Soap washes clothes cleanest. *Y*__ __ *t*__ __ can look like a super model. Just a *f*__ __ squirts and *s*__ __ __ your clothes will look like *n*__ __. *U*__ __ Super Soap *t*__ wash all your clothes.

8. A small family of words end in **ue**. Write the words that fit these clues:

something sticky	**gl__ __**
colour of the sky	**bl__ __**
you need it to solve a mystery	**cl__ __**
not false but	**tr__ __**
what the actor waits for	**c__ __**

9. The Challenge Words **fruit** and **suit** belong to a small group of words. Fill in the missing letters below and use your words in the sentences that follow.

fr__ __t   s__ __t   br__ __se   cr__ __se   j__ __ce

If the __ __ __ __ __ gets a __ __ __ __ __ __ you can squeeze it and make __ __ __ __ __.

He wore his new __ __ __ __ on the __ __ __ __ __ __.

10. Write the four common words that end in long *u* spelled **o**:

    wh__   **d__**   **t__**   **int__**

11. When do you use the Challenge Word **into**? When there is action or movement **in to** something.

    I am _____ trouble. (**in, into**)
    You are walking _____ danger! (**in, into**)
    The idea came _____ my mind. (**in, into**)
    The man went out _____ the freezing cold night, closing the door behind him. (**in, into**)
    We're _____ the kitchen. (**in, into**)
    Look deep _____ my eyes. (**in, into**)

Home Connections

Word play and nonsense are important parts of learning to read, write, and spell. Get your child to think up nonsense words that fit the patterns. For example, to the **oom** wheel, he could add: **kaboom, throom, choom, vroom**, and make up meanings for them. Or teach him this silly tongue twister:

A tutor who tootled the flute
Was teaching two tooters to toot.
Said the two to the tutor,
"Is it harder to toot,
Or to tutor two tooters to toot?"

Cartoonists make up words all the time. Read "Calvin and Hobbes" or "Archie" with your child and look for neat words the authors have invented.

3 Other Vowel Patterns

Other Vowel Patterns

Introduction

Once the long vowel patterns are familiar, children can begin to learn other vowel sounds and their spellings. For example, the first part of Section 3 teaches what we call the **r–controlled vowels**. When a vowel is followed by an **r** the sound changes slightly. For example:

pat becomes **part**

pot becomes **port**

Your child needs to recognize that the *er* sound, which is very common, can be spelled: **er** (**farmer**, **her**), **ir** (**dirt**, **sir**), **ur** (**hurt**, **burn**), or **or** (**doctor**, **worm**).

Clearly, we cannot rely on sound to spell words with the *er* sound, but need tactics to remember what these words look like. It can help to group them in smaller patterns. For example, many *er* sound words that begin with **w** use the **or** spelling: w**or**m, w**or**d, w**or**th, w**or**ld, and w**or**k.

Next, Section 3 works with other vowel patterns such as the **oo** in **book**; the **oy** in **boy**; and the **ow** in **how**.

The last unit in the section tackles the ticklish business of "i before e, except after c." Words with the **ie** combination can be difficult, but when they are grouped according to sound, spelling, and meaning they are much easier to remember. For example, in words such as **eight** and **vein** the **ei** spelling has the sound of long **a**. This fits the old spelling rhyme:

i before **e**, except after **c**, or

when it says **a**, as in

neighbour and **weigh**.

UNIT 15

Short *a* + *r*; Short *o* + *r*

Dictate the list saying each word clearly but naturally. Use a sentence to make the meaning clear.

Unit Words

car	They had to jump out of the way of the speeding **car.**
for	I got a new camera **for** my birthday.
or	Watch your step **or** you might fall.
park	We played ball in the **park** down the street.
four	I went on that ride **four** times in a row.
more	There is **more** than one parrot in the cage.
your	What's **your** favourite food?
door	Lewis slowly opened the **door**.
morning	The **morning** light shone through the window.

roar	You could hear the engine's **roar** from far away.
shark	Are you sure there isn't a **shark** in your pool?
farm	Pigs are my favourite **farm** animal.
store	The **store** is three blocks away.
March	My birthday is in the month of **March**.
board	There was a **board** missing from the floor.

Challenge Words

war	My grandfather fought in the **war**.
warm	Thank goodness for **warm** weather!
are	Where **are** my shoes?
heart	The valentine was in the shape of a **heart**.
before	I shared a room with my sister **before** I moved.

Your child can learn a lot by comparing misspellings to the correct form. For example, if he writes **shak** for **shark**, you can point out the difficult *r* sound, making sure he can hear it.

We call **ar** and **or** r-controlled vowels because the **r** changes the sound of the vowels slightly.

Rewrite any misspelled words.

dictation	rewrite
shak	shark

What's the Secret?

1. Say these pairs of words. Listen to the sounds of *a* and *ar*. Are the sounds the same or different?

cat—cart
pat—part
ban—barn
am—arm

2. Say the pairs of words below. Listen to the sound of *o* and *or*. What happens to the short *o* when **r** is added?

spot—sport   con—corn
shot—short   ton—torn

3. Look at the words below. Underline the letters that spell the **or** sound in each word.

for   your   roar   more   court

Spelling Secret #15
R-controlled Vowels
Short **a** followed by **r** sounds like *ar* as in **car**. It is almost always spelled **ar**: **car, park, farm**.
Short **o** followed by **r** sounds like *or* as in **for**. The short **or** has several spellings. The most common are: **or** (for), **ore** (store), **oar** (roar), **our** (four).

Putting the Secret to Work

The exercise on rhyme helps your child hear the difference between **pat** and **part**.

1. Which words rhyme? Say each pair of words below. Write the pairs that rhyme and underline the rhyming parts.

start—cart	**hard—had**	**shot—short**
cat—cart	**hard—yard**	**fort—form**
pat—part	**yard—yarn**	**fort—short**

Some words beginning with **w** have the **ar** spelling pronounced *or*, as in **war**, **ward**, **warm**, **warn**. Watch out for those **w**'s!

2. Complete the circles. Say each word as you write it and listen for the *ar* sound.

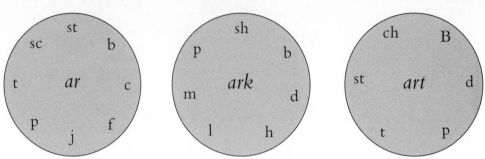

3. Write three rhyming words for each **ar** pattern below:

arm	f_____	h_____	ch_____
ard	gu_____	h_____	y_____
arch	M_____	st_____	p_____
arp	c_____	h_____	sh_____
arge	ch_____	b_____	l_____

4. Write the Unit Words, filling in the missing letters.

p__ __k   sh__ __k   f__ __m   M__ __ch

Once again, your child will need to look at the words closely and learn their shape and appearance, as well as their sound.

Use the words in these sentences.

We had fun on the swings in the __ ◯__ __.

There are pigs and chickens on the __ __◯__.

His birthday is in __ __ __◯__.

I see a huge __◯__ __ __ in the water!

Now use the circled letters to answer this riddle:

Q. What holds up your foot and a building?

A. An __ __ __ __.

Word Families with *or*

There are many interesting and useful words with **or**, from **roar** to **enormous**. There are also several different spelling patterns for this sound.

5. Write the rhyming words around each circle. Say each word and listen for the *or* sound.

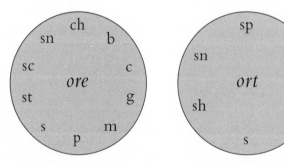

6. Write three rhyming words for each **or** pattern below.

orm	st_____	f_____	N_____
our	f_____	p_____	y_____
oar	s_____	r_____	b_____
orn	b_____	t_____	w_____

7. Write two words that rhyme with **bore** but spell **or** with **oor**.
I walked through the *d__ __ __* and fell on the *fl__ __ __*.

8. Unscramble the Unit Words with **or** that fit these sentences.

What is __ __ __ __ name?	**o y u r**
The lion had a very loud __ __ __ __.	**a r o r**
He hammered a nail into the __ __ __ __ __.	**o b a r d**
What did you buy at the __ __ __ __ __?	**t o r s e**
It was a beautiful __ __ __ __ __ __ __.	**g m r o n i n**
She opened the __ __ __ __ and let the dog in.	**o d o r**
The table has __ __ __ __ legs.	**o f u r**
Do you want some __ __ __ __?	**e r o m**

*Heart is a hard word. You can remember that you **hear** your **heart** beat.*

9. Write the Challenge Words, filling in the blank letters.
w__ __m   w__ __   __ __e
h__ __ __t   bef__ __ __

10. Write the Challenge Words that fit these clues:
◯__ __ __ This word means the opposite of **cool** and spells **or** with **ar**.
◯__ __ __ __ This word spells **ar** with **ear**.
◯__ __This word has three letters and sounds like the name of the letter **r**.
__ __◯ This word also spells **or** with **ar** and means an armed conflict between countries.
__ __◯__ __ __ This word has two syllables and spells **or** with **ore**.
The letters in the circles spell a word that means a place boats dock. It has the *or* sound spelled **ar** <u>and</u> a silent *h*!

__ __ __ __ __

For and four are important words for your child to spell correctly. More about homonyms in Unit 31.

11. For and **four** sound the same, but they have different meanings and spellings. To spell the right word you have to think about the meaning. Use the correct word in these sentences.
She studied _____ an hour.
How much do you want _____ that dog?
I think it is almost _____ o'clock.
He is going to the store _____ me.
My little brother is _____ years old.

Home Connections
Dictionary Skills
We use alphabetical order almost every day of our lives. If you're at the mall looking at a directory, have your child notice how the stores are grouped. If you're looking for a doctor's office in the directory of a large medical building, notice if the doctors' names are listed alphabetically.

Guide Words

In large books such as telephone directories and dictionaries, guide words at the top of the page help you find out if you're on the right page at a glance. For example, if you want **corn**, you'll find it on the page with **cauliflower** on one side and **cottage** on the other, since **cor** comes after **ca** and before **cot**.

Encyclopedias and some atlases also use guide words. Practise looking up names in phone books, words in dictionaries, or topics in encyclopedias using the guide words. For example:

Will you find **elephant** on this page in the encyclopedia?

eggplant	Europe

UNIT 16

Dictate the list. Be sure to give your child time to write each word.

Short *e* + *r* sound: *er*, *ir*, *ur*, and *or*

Unit Words

her	What is **her** name?
bird	His favourite **bird** is a bluejay.
work	We have to **work** hard at school.
turn	Please **turn** off the stove.
girl	This **girl** is my sister.
first	Heather was the **first** in line.
after	What are you doing **after** school?
water	The **water** in the pool was cold!
word	Do you know how to spell that **word**?
ever	Have you **ever** been to Ottawa?
better	This movie is **better** than the last one.
surprise	What a great **surprise**!
doctor	The **doctor** will help you get well.
purple	He was wearing a **purple** jacket.
never	I have **never** seen that man before.

Challenge Words

heard★
learn
birthday
dollars

★One of the 25 most frequently misspelled words

Check the Pretest with your child. Encourage her to do her own marking and to notice which letters she had wrong. Emphasize the letters she spelled correctly too!

We call **e** followed by **r** an *r*-controlled vowel.

Were you at the store yesterday?
We **heard** the song on the radio.
How can we **learn** to play that music?
My **birthday** is on Saturday.
He had twenty **dollars** in the bank.

Rewrite any misspelled words.

What's the Secret?

1. Say each pair of words. What happens to the sound of short *e* when we add **r**?
   bet—Bert   pet—pert

2. Say these words. What sound do you hear in the middle of each? Underline the letters that spell **er**.
   bird   word   turn   fern   her   sir   fur

3. Write these two-syllable words. What do you notice about the **er** sound at the end?
   farmer   doctor   better   dollars

> ### Spelling Secret #16
> The sound of short *e* and *r* can be spelled **er**, **ur**, **ir**, or sometimes **or** in one-syllable words: **bird, her, work, turn**.
> The *er* sound is usually spelled **er** at the end of longer words: **water, better, after**. Other spellings are **or** and **ar**: **doctor, dollars**.
> We need to remember how the word looks to spell the sound *er* correctly.

Have your child say each word in the puzzle aloud. Ask what sound the letters **or** make.

Putting the Secret to Work

1. Write the Unit Word with **er** that matches each clue.

many fly south for the winter	d r i b
If you have a new niece, the baby is a	l g r i
If there's a flood, there's too much of it	t r e w a
To win a gold medal you must be	i s f r t

2. Write the words with **or** that fit the definitions. One is a Unit Word.

a long wiggly creature	w	__	__	m
something hard to do	w	__	__	k
the planet earth is our____	w	__	__	ld
it's bad and getting _____	w	__	__	se
how much is it _____?	w	__	__	th
it's bad, it's worse, it's the ____	w	__	__	st

OTHER VOWEL PATTERNS   **61**

Surprise is a difficult word to spell because we don't hear the first **r**. Also, many children want to spell it **surprize** because they have already learned **prize** with a **z**. Have your child write the word with blanks for the hard letters: s __ __ pri __ e.

I've never seen a purple cow
I never want to see one

But I can tell you, here and now,
I'd rather see, than be one!

A few words end in **or**: **doctor**, **actor**, **visitor**, **instructor**.

Some common words spell **er** with **ar**: **dollar**, **collar**, **beggar**, **grammar**.

Earth and search are two more common words that spell **er** with **ear**.

3. Fill in the blanks to write these Unit Words. Use a different colour for each of **er, ur, or**.

h__ __
t__ __n, s __ __ prise
aft__ __ , bett__ __
ev__ __, nev__ __
doct__ __
p__ __ple

4. Use the Unit Words above in these sentences.
If I don't get my *t__ __ n* soon, I'm going to burst!
I want to see my *s __ __ __ __ __ __ __*!
You'll feel *b__ __ __ __ __ a__ __ __ __* you see the *d__ __ __ __ __*.
I have *n__ __ __ __* seen *h__ __* wearing *p__ __ __ __ __*.
Have you *e__ __ __* talked to my teacher?

5. When we add **er** to the end of an action word (verb) we make the name of a person who does that action. A **walker** walks. Write the names of people who do these things.
I **sing**. I'm a __ __ __ __ __ __.
I **play** basketball. I'm a basketball __ __ __ __ __ __.
I **work**. I'm a __ __ __ __ __ __.
I **teach**. I'm a __ __ __ __ __ __ __.
I **wait** on tables in a restaurant. I'm a __ __ __ __ __ __.

6. Unscramble these Challenge Words. Look at the way **er** is spelled in each one. Why do you think **were** and **heard** are two of the most often misspelled words?

adreh   rwee   llrsoda
raeln   ybidrhat

7. Write the Challenge Words that fit these sentences.
We *h__ __ __d* a new song on the radio.
I hope I can *l__ __ __n* to speak French.
Where *w__ __e* you yesterday?
She got a puppy for her *b__ __ thday*.
It cost two hundred *doll__ __ s*.

8. Look for these **er** sound words in the **Word Search**

er	ir	ur
together	shirt	hurt
supper	skirt	turtle
under	third	church
winter	sir	curb
summer	stir	blur
herd	dirt	fur
older		
silver		

b	s	u	p	p	e	r	a	w	c
b	r	u	c	r	u	l	b	i	c
r	e	d	m	s	t	i	r	n	h
e	l	e	g	m	h	j	k	t	u
v	t	t	o	g	e	t	h	e	r
l	r	h	u	r	t	r	e	r	c
i	u	i	f	p	r	i	r	e	h
s	t	r	i	d	i	s	d	d	l
o	l	d	e	r	h	i	o	n	n
t	r	i	k	s	s	m	f	u	r

Home Connections

Have your child look for words with the *er* sound in books, newspapers, signs and on TV. She needs to learn how these words look. Try to connect the meaning to the spelling whenever possible.

For example:

What do you **hear** with?

I **hear** with my **ear**.

The past tense **heard** follows the spelling pattern of **hear** and **ear** but changes the sound.

Too means also or more than enough. For example:

too many people

too much candy

too much snow

too many cats

Your child can remember the **o's** in **too** because there are **too** many!

UNIT 17

Long *er* and *ar*

Use your own sentences for dictation whenever they will help make a word meaning especially clear. For example: "Take good care of (use the name of a brother, sister, pet, toy)."

Unit Words

ear	These pills are for my **ear** infection.
air	All the **air** rushed out of the balloon.
here	**Here** is a letter for you.
care	Take good **care** of your new skates.
hear	I can **hear** the music very clearly.

years	How many **years** have you been going to school?
bear	The brown **bear** scooped a fish out of the stream.
cheer	There was a huge **cheer** when he hit a home run.
hair	Her **hair** was brown and curly.
clear	This is a nice **clear** picture of the mountains.
bare	The trees look very **bare** without any leaves.
stairs	How many **stairs** are there from here to the ground?
scare	You can't **scare** me with that silly mask!
appear	The full moon will **appear** about eight o'clock.
parent	You have to go to that show with a **parent**.

Challenge Words

very	She did **very** well on her math test.
where★	**Where** did you get that chocolate bar?
their★	I really like **their** new friends.
there	What is over **there** on the hill?
marry	My sister is going to **marry** that man next week.

★One of the 25 most frequently misspelled words

Check the Pretest with your child.

Rewrite any misspelled words.

Sph as in **sphere** is an unusual consonant combination, but **sphere** is a word your child will meet in mathematics. Have your child listen for the way in which **ph** sounds like *f.*

What's the Secret?

1. Make a chart like the one below. Write the following words under the right heading:

fear   **beer**   **here**   **steer**   **year**   **sphere**

ear	ere	eer

2. Say the following pairs of words aloud. What letter do we add to the ends of words to make the **ar** sound long?

scar—scare   car—care   bar—bare

3. Say these pairs aloud. What vowel do we add to make the **ar** long?

star—stair   far—fair

The contraction **they're** (for **they are**) also sounds like **their** and **there**. It is taught in Unit 30, but if your child knows the word, you may want to include it here. For example, "They're going over there to pick up their daughter."

Spelling Secret #17

The long *er* sound is spelled **ear** in words such as **ear, clear, appear**.
Long *er* can also be spelled **eer** as in **cheer**.
The long **ar** sound is spelled **air** in words such as **air, hair**, and **stairs**.
Long *ar* can also be spelled **are** in words such as **care, scare**, and **parent**.

Putting the Secret to Work

Rhyming words with long *er*

1. Complete the word wheels with **ear** and **eer** words. Say each word as you write it and underline the rhyming parts.

Notice that some words with ear rhyme with **air**: **bear**, **pear**, **wear**, **tear**. To add to the confusion there are two words spelled **tear**: I have a **tear** in my eye. **Tear** up the paper.

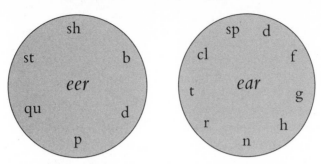

2. Unscramble the Unit Words with long *er* that fit these definitions.

Not cloudy or confused.	**l r a e c**
Something you do at a ball game.	**r c e h e**
One on each side of your head.	**r a e**
It sounds exactly like **hear**.	**e h r e**
There are 365 1/4 days in each one of these.	**s y r a e**
If you call her name, she will _____.	**p r a p e a**

3. Here and **hear** and **deer** and **dear** are homonyms. They mean different things and look different, but they sound the same. Fill in the words that fit the meanings of these sentences.

__ __ __ __ I am! Over __ __ __ __. Can't you __ __ __ __ me? I can __ __ __ __ you very clearly!

The animal was a __ __ __ __ little faun. Its mother, a full grown __ __ __ __, stood beside it. Oh __ __ __ __! It ran away before I could take a picture!

Rhyming words with long *ar*

4. Complete the shapes with words that rhyme with **air**. Underline the rhyming parts.

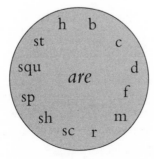 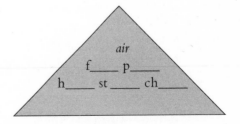

5. Many useful words end in the long *ar* sound. Some of these are homonyms—they sound the same but look different. Use the correct one in the sentences below.

I will pay your *f* _____ to the *f*_____.   fare—fair

That big Arctic *h* _____ has a lot of *h*_____.   hare—hair

Everyone *s* _____ at the purple *s*_____.   stares—stairs

A good way to remember how to spell **their** and **there** is that they both begin with **the**.

6. Write the Challenge Words, filling in the missing letters. Say the words. What sound do you hear in each?

wh__ __ __   th__ __r   th__ __ __   v__ __ y   m__ __ __y

We use **there** when we mean a position or place as in: **There** is my baseball glove. or It's over **there**. We also use **there** when we are pointing something out as in: **There** are over forty stores in the mall.

7. We use **their** when we mean belonging to them.
Use **their** or **there** in these sentences.

_____ are sixteen girls and nineteen boys in _____ class.

_____ friends are over _____.

_____ is the baseball team, but where are _____ uniforms?

Writing the letters in different ways is a good way to focus on the word.

8. Very is a word you need to remember by sight. Try writing it four different ways:

• with the **er** in big fat letters
• with the **er** in tall, skinny letters
• with the **er** in capitals
• in your own special and memorable way!

9. The word **marry** belongs to a small family. You can remember this word with a silly sentence:

Your child may notice that the girl's name **Mary** has only one **r**.

Harry will **marry** a girl who will **carry** him up to the church.
Fill in the triangle with **arry** words:

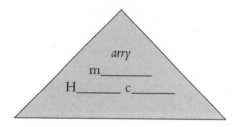

Home Connections

Play word games such as Scrabble® and Spill and Spell® with your child to develop "word sense."

If you have a home computer, you can also play games such as *Family Feud* or *Jeopardy*. Team up as partners against the computer teams. These games strengthen spelling skills because they will only recognize and accept an answer that is spelled correctly. And your child gets to see the correctly spelled word on the screen soon after his "try." Games such as these reinforce the idea that correct spelling matters in many real life situations.

However, encourage your child to write first drafts of stories, poems, and other creative writing projects without stopping to worry if every word is correctly spelled while they're trying to put their fleeting thoughts on paper. For most children, the ability to express ideas and feelings outstrips their spelling ability at the beginning. Reinforce proofreading—checking carefully to make sure spelling is correct—before they do a final draft.

UNIT 18

Vowel Sounds: *ow* as in *how*; *oy* as in *boy*

Dictate the Unit and Challenge Words. Using sentences for words such as **our** and **hour** helps make their meanings clear.

Unit Words

out	Let the dog **out**, please.
boy	Our youngest **boy** is off to camp.
our★	Where is **our** pet snake?
about	The story was **about** an enormous giant.
down	She looked deep **down** into the well.
house	They say that **house** was built a hundred years ago.
join	Would you like to **join** our club?
now	We are supposed to be there **now**.
how	**How** are we going to find out his phone number?
found	I **found** this shell in Florida.
soil	We bought some **soil** to plant our flowers.
brown	Most of the people in my class have **brown** hair.
hour	**Hour** after **hour** passed and still no phone call!
mouse	Put the trap right in front of the **mouse** hole.
around	I've looked all **around** for my present.

Challenge Words

voice	His **voice** was very loud.
without	She knocked **without** hesitation.
noise	What's all that **noise**?
annoy	My brother loves to **annoy** me!
outside	The house was very tidy **outside** and in.

★One of the 25 most frequently misspelled words.

Check the pretest. Have your child rewrite the misspelled words, underlining the misspelled letters.

What's the Secret?

1. Say each of the words below. Write each word and circle the letters that say *ow* as in **how**.

    brown   **town**   **gown**

Say each of these words. Write each word and underline the letters that say *ow* as in **how**.

    about   **shout**   **count**

2. Write each word and circle the vowels. Say each word. What sound do you hear?

    boy   **joy**

Write these words. Underline the letters that say *oy* as in **boy.**

    join   **coin**   **soil**   **toil**   **voice**   **choice**

> ### Spelling Secret #18
> Words with the sound *ow* as in **how** are spelled: **ow (clown, now, cow);** or **ou (loud, house, found).**
> Words with the sound *oy* as in **boy** are spelled: **oy (boy, toy, joy);** or **oi (oil, join, voice).**

Putting the Secret to Work

Rhyming words with *ow* as in *how*

1. Complete the circles below. Say each word and circle the rhyming part.

Remind your child that in many words, **ow** spells long *o*, as in **know** and **snow**. A word like snowplow contains both sounds of *ow*.

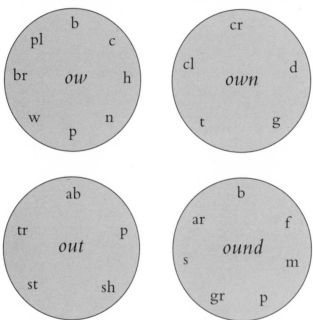

2. Write the three-letter word that is the name of a large bird.

    __ __l

Write four words that rhyme with **owl.**

    h____   **sc**____   **pr**____   **gr**____

3. Write a five-letter Unit Word that is the name of a small animal.

    m__ __ __ __

Write three more words that rhyme with mouse.

    h____   **l**____   **gr**____

Many people pronounce **our** to rhyme with **jar**. Maybe that's why this small word is one of the most often misspelled in our language.

4. Solve this puzzle by writing Unit Words that fit the blanks.

My cat wants to go ◯__ __. Open the door.

You can't go out n__◯ I'm busy.

◯__ __ last names sound the same.

She fell d__◯__ the stairs.

The kids ran __◯__ __ __ __ the circle.

The big hand on the clock tells you the h◯__ __.

She has dark b__ __◯__ hair.

I'm glad I f__ __◯__ my lost wallet.

Their h◯__ __ __ has six rooms.

__ __◯ many kids go to our school?

Use the letters in the circles to ask an old nursery rhyme question.

Answer:

H__ __ n__ __, b__ __ __ __ c__ __?

5. Say the words **our** and **hour** with your child. Are they homonyms for you? According to many dictionaries, they are pronounced the same way. The **h** in **hour** is silent.

Write the words in this sentence.

__ __ __ clock is over an __ __ __ __ slow.

Rhyming words with *oy*

6. Complete the triangles. Say each word as you write it and circle the letters that spell **oy**.

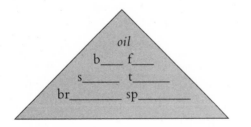

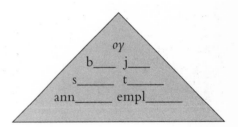

7. Write the Unit and Challenge Words that rhyme with:

coin—j__ __n   choice—v__ __ ce   poise—n__ __ se

8. News Headlines. Unscramble the Unit and Challenge Words that fit these newspaper headlines.

> NEIGHBOURS **NJIO** PROTEST AGAINST NEW AIRPORT
> LOUD **SNEIO** WILL **YNAON** RESIDENTS
> **YBO** FINDS DINOSAUR BONE BURIED IN **LSOI**
> NEW COMPUTER GAMES ACTIVATED BY **CEIOV** COMMANDS

Words made up of two smaller words are called compound words. More about compounds in Unit 22.

9. Two of the Challenge Words contain the word **out**. Complete the words by adding the missing vowels.

w__th__ __t   __ __ts__d__

10. Word Explosion. Write longer words by adding **out**. Underline **out** in each word.

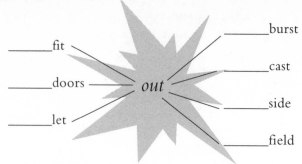

_____fit

_____doors

_____let

out

_____burst

_____cast

_____side

_____field

Home Connections

Have your child look in the dictionary for more words beginning with **out**. Use the guide words at the top of the pages to help you. (For example, the *Gage Junior Dictionary* has more than two full pages of **out** words, from **out** to **out-stretched**.)

Here's an old riddle with **out**:
Black within and red without
Four corners round about.
What am I?

UNIT 19

Dictate the words and have your child write them in a list.

More Vowel Patterns: *ŭ* as in *put*

Unit Words

took	I **took** the cookies off the shelf.
mother	I live with my **mother** and sister.
good	This should be a **good** day for skiing!
other	Where's my **other** shoe?
look	**Look** under the bed for your shoe.
father	My **father** loves to fish.
put	Don't **put** your nose where it doesn't belong!
book	I read that **book** in five days.
bought	Sandra just **bought** a new pair of boots.
push	I guess we will have to **push** the car.
should	He **should** be coming out that door any minute.
thought	It was Chris who **thought** of a way out.
would	Where **would** you like to go?
brought	Henry's dog **brought** back the stick.
could	He **could** have called while I was out.

Challenge Words

because★
caught★
months
another★
enough

★One of the 25 most frequently misspelled words.

Check the dictation. Notice that **because**, **another**, and **caught** are all frequently misspelled words. If your child had trouble with these words, highlight them for special attention.

b e c a u s e

I'll have to wash my coat **because** I fell in the mud.
Don't get **caught** in the act.
It's been **months** since I had my hair cut.
We are going to put **another** picture on that wall.
I have **enough** time to finish the test.

What's the Secret?

1. Look at the words below. Say each word. What vowel sound do you hear? Dictionaries often list this sound as a *u* with a dot over it—**u̇**. It is the sound of *u* in **put**.

    took   good   look   wood

Say each word. What vowel sound do you hear? Which two letters spell this sound?

    should   could

2. Say each of these words. Which letters spell the short **o** sound?

    bought   brought   thought

3. Say these words. Which letter spells the short **u** sound?

    other   mother   months

Spelling Secret #19

The sound *u̇* as in **put** is often spelled **u**: **put**, **push**, **pull**.
The *u̇* sound can also be spelled **oo** as in **look** or **book**, or **ou** as in **could** or **would**.
The short *o* as in **hot** can be spelled **ough** or **augh** as in **bought**, **brought**, **caught**, **taught**.

Putting the Secret to Work

Rhyming Families with *u̇* as in *put*

Have your child say the words **flood** and **blood** and notice the different sound of *oo*. Here it sounds like the short *u*, as in **but**.

1. Complete the circles with rhyming words spelled with **oo**. Say each word as you write it.

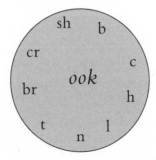
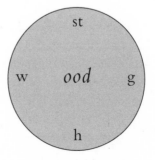

Both the long *u* spelled **oo** and the sound *u* as in **book** are common patterns.

2. Which words rhyme? Sort the **oo** words into two columns.

brook, good, zoo, pool, boom, zoom, soon, wood, shook, too, stool, food

oo as in t**oo**k	**oo** as in t**u**ne

3. Unscramble these silly mixed-up Unit Words with **ů** to make sense out of these sentences.

She **koto** a **kolo** at that new **kobo**.

Don't **suhp**!

He **upt** on a bike helmet.

He is a **doog-kool**ing guy!

Sometimes an old rhyme can help children remember hard words that are spelled the same: I **would** if I **could** but I can't, so I won't!

Remind your child of the silent **gh** in words such as **light** in Unit 12.

4. Look at **would, could,** and **should**:

Which letters spell *ů* as in **put**? __ __

Which letter is silent? __

Fill in the blanks in this rhyme.

I *w*__ __ __*d* help if I *c*__ __ __*d*.

And I know I really *sh*__ __ __*d*.

5. Look at **brought, thought, bought,** and **fought**.

Which letters spell short *o* as in **hot**? __ __

Which letters are silent? __ __ __

Use the words to finish these sentences.

Let me see what you *b*__ __ __ __ __ at the mall.

I *th*__ __ __ __ __ you were going to the movies.

We *br*__ __ __ __ __ you a present.

My grandfather *f*__ __ __ __ __ in the war.

6. Complete the family words:

Words for members of a family all end in **er** except one, and that word is **son**.

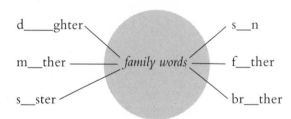

d____ghter

m__ther

s__ster

family words

s__n

f__ther

br__ther

7. Write the two Unit Words that are names for people in a family.

m__th__ __   f__th__ __

Write the Unit Word that rhymes with **mother**.

br__ __ __ __ __

8. Focus on the Challenge Word **because**. It's easier to spell if you break it into two syllables.

be•cause

The **be** is easy! Which letters are hard to remember? Write the word with blanks for the vowels five times.

bec__ __se

bec__ __se

bec__ __se

bec__ __se

bec__ __se

Now think of five interesting ways to write **au**—tall, fat, in different colours, on a slant, or in capital letters.

9. Write the Challenge Word that:

- sounds like **cot** but has four letters between **c** and **t**. c__ __ __ __t
- rhymes with **brother** an__ __ __ __ __
- ends with **ths**, a hard sound to say! m__ __ths
- ends with **gh** pronounced like **f** en__ __ __ __

10. aught is found in the words **taught** and **caught**. You need to remember how these words look as well as their sound.

teach—taught

catch—caught

Yesterday she t__ __ __ __t him where to find fishing worms. Today she will t__ __ __h him how to put the worm on the hook. He hopes he will c__ __ __h a fish. Yesterday all he c__ __ __ __t was an old boot!

Home Connections

Some patterns like **look, cook, took** are large. Others, such as **mother, brother,** and **other** have only a few words. Still, the rhyming patterns can help children remember how to spell them.

Have your child list patterns in a spelling binder, especially interesting patterns such as:

flood	**caught**	**enough**	**brought**
blood	**taught**	**tough**	**thought**
		rough	**fought**

He can add patterns as they are discovered. This will be increasingly important as words get longer and more complex. Suggest using a page or a half page for each pattern and illustrate the words or write sentences or rhymes to help remember. For example:

enough	The wolf was big **enough**
rough	and **rough enough**
tough	and **tough enough** to blow the little pig's house down with one **puff**!

Many children get **month** and **mouth** confused. Have them practise saying the words, listening for the *n* sound in **month** and the *ou* (**ow**! as in **how**) sound in **mouth**.

Dictate the Unit and Challenge Words. Since this is a Pretest of some difficult words, don't have your child puzzle too long over how to spell a word.

"*i* before *e*, except after *c*"

Unit Words

field	The farmer planted corn in the **field**.
thief	That **thief** stole money from the bank.
fierce	I'm afraid of big **fierce** dogs!
deceive	They can't **deceive** me—I know it's not real!
niece	My sister's baby girl is my **niece**.
movie	She loved that **movie** so much she went twice.
yield	There is a **yield** sign at the corner.
receive	When will you **receive** the package from your aunt?
ceiling	The **ceiling** was falling down around us.
piece	I want a big **piece** of pie.
vein	She discovered a thick **vein** of silver in the rock.
weigh	How much does he **weigh**?
believe	I don't **believe** you're telling me the truth!
eight	Her little sister is **eight** years old.
neighbour	My **neighbour** has a swimming pool.

Challenge Words

either	I want **either** a milkshake or a sundae.
neither	**Neither** of those boys is my friend.
height	What is the **height** of that skyscraper?
seize	The police officer will **seize** the stolen goods.
science	My favourite subject is **science**.

Check the pretest with your child, paying special attention to the **ie** and **ei** combinations.

What's the Secret?

1. Write these Unit Words in the correct column below.
field, vein, piece, niece, weigh, thief, eight, neighbour, yield, movie, believe

ie pronounced long *e*	**ei** pronounced long *a*

2. Say these words. How is the long *e* sound spelled?
receive, deceive, ceiling, conceited
Which letter comes before the **ei** spelling? _____
Write each word and circle **cei**.

Some other words where long *e* is spelled **ie** are: **shield, wield; grieve, brief; grief, cookie; belief**.

Putting the Secret to Work

1. Solve the puzzle by writing Unit Words with **ie** that fit the clues.

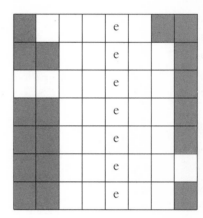

Another name for a robber is a

A piece of ground where things grow is a

When you have beliefs, you

If something is delicious, you want a big

When you give in, you

Very wild, possibly scary is

Your brother or sister's daughter is your

Do all the words in the puzzle follow the "**i** before **e**, except after **c**" rule?
Yes ☐   **No** ☐

2. Fill in the vowels to write these words.

rec__ __ve   rec__ __pt   c__ __ling

dec__ __ve   dec__ __t   conc__ __t

Do they follow the rule "**i** before **e**, except after **c**"?
Yes ☐   **No** ☐

Point out the silent *p* in **receipt**. This is a truly tricky spelling!

3. Match each word below to its definition.

receive	too much pride in oneself
ceiling	the top covering of a room
conceit	take something, be given
receipt	make someone believe something untrue
deceive	a written statement that money or a letter was received

4. Unscramble the Unit Words that fit the Heavy Headlines.

> GIANT **NIVE** OF GOLD DISCOVERED IN **EINHBGSR'UO** BACKYARD
> HUGE PUMPKIN WILL **GIHEW** AS MUCH AS A HOUSE
> FREIGHT CARS WILL BRING **GETIH** ELEPHANTS TO CIRCUS

5. Fill in the vowels to write these Unit Words.

    n__ __ghbour   __ __ght   w__ __gh   v__ __n

Do all these words follow the "**i** before **e**, except after **c**" rule?

    Yes ☐   **No** ☐

Some other words where long *a* is spelled **ei** are: **neigh** (the sound a horse makes), **neighbour, sleigh, reindeer, rein** (on a horse), **reign** (the rule of a king or queen), **eighteen, eighth, eighty, veil, weight**.

Challenge Words with *ie*

6. Four of the Challenge Words are exceptions to the "**i** before **e**" rule. You need to learn how they **look**, not how they sound. Write the words below filling in the vowels.

    __ __ther   n__ __ther
    h__ __ght   s__ __ze

7. Unscramble the Challenge Words to fit these sentences.

    Nazim gets good marks in **c i n e c s e**.
    You must **z e i s e** the rope with both hands.
    She is **t i h e n r e** thin or fat.
    He said, "**h t r i e e** you or I will have to go!"
    What is the **g t i h e h** of that tower?

8. Write the Challenge Word with a silent *c* before **ie**.

    s__ __ __nce

    Science has two syllables: **sci•ence**.

    The long *i* belongs to the first syllable.

    The short *e* belongs to the second syllable.

A memory trick for learning the **c** in **science** is to pronounce the first **c** as a *k*: s*k*ience.

Home Connections

If you haven't done so already, try to set aside a special place in your home for your child to write and work on spelling. It doesn't have to be in an isolated corner, just far away enough from distractions such as TV so that he can concentrate.

Keep a good dictionary, a notebook, plenty of paper, pencils and pens, coloured markers and highlighters handy. A bulletin board to tack up lists of words, messages, or your child's writing is also a good idea.

For travelling, you can make a spelling kit, with writing materials, word cards, word search and word puzzle books, a pocket dictionary, and any word games that are small enough to be portable.

Either and **neither** can be pronounced with long *e* or long *i*. Both are correct.

Some other exceptions to the **ie** words are: **weird, leisure, foreign, sheik.**

4 Word Building

Word Building

Introduction

Sections 1, 2, and 3 of *Sharing the Secrets* dealt with the many patterns involving the link between sounds and letters. While it is important to understand these patterns, this knowledge alone will not make someone a good speller. As children grow in their ability to handle language concepts, they begin to realize that many words are not spelled just the way they sound. For example, if the word **jumped** were sounded out it should be spelled **jumpt**. This is, in fact, how many young children spell the word. Gradually, however, they come to understand that when a word is made into the past tense, meaning it happened in the past, the ending used is "ed." There are exceptions, of course, as in **come**—**came**, but this rule works most of the time.

Changing a verb from the present to the past tense is a form of *word building*. There are many other rules involving making a change to a base word. These patterns include combining words into compound words, making words plural, showing possession, forming contractions, adding endings such as "ed" and "ing," and so forth.

Some children seem to pick up these rules very naturally through their reading and writing. These fortunate ones are usually also good readers and have a general strength in the area of language. For many children, however, a rich reading and writing environment is not enough to ensure that these spelling rules will be understood. In addition to having many opportunities to read and write, these children also need some formal instruction to help them see the patterns.

Section 4 of this book deals with the basic rules for word building beyond the level of phonics. Old spelling texts usually presented such rules in a complicated fashion at the beginning of the lesson, and assumed that the child would understand, memorize, and apply the rule with ease. We now know that when presented in this way, such rules often seem like gibberish, and show little or no transference to the child's actual writing. As in Sections 1, 2, and 3, we have structured each unit so that the child is led to discover each pattern through examining the unit words and answering a systematic set of questions in the "What's the Secret?" section. The rule is then stated clearly as a "Spelling Secret," and applied in "Putting the Secret to Work."

This section is suitable for Grade 4 and up.

It is important to realize that your child may or may not be ready for this level of patterning. For the most part, children in Grade 4 and up will be able to work successfully in this part of the book. Your child, however, may need more time before he or she can understand and use these rules. Be patient, and do not push too hard. It is better to go away from the book for a few weeks and concentrate on reviewing simpler patterns than to frustrate your child with concepts that are too advanced. You may be pleasantly surprised in a few months to discover that your child easily grasps patterns that had seemed so difficult just a short time before.

Sections 4, 5, and 6 are set up so that the child takes more and more responsibility for working independently on the unit. You should still be involved, however, in talking about each rule and making sure your child is clear about the pattern. Watch to see whether the practice with the Secret is done correctly. If not, your child might still be confused about the rule. There are additional lists of words that fit each pattern in Appendix II if you feel extra work is needed. Also pay close attention to the suggestions in "Home Connections." These ideas will help you to assess how well your child understands the pattern for the unit, while having fun at the same time! Gradually, you should see these rules being applied in your child's everyday writing. If they are not, discuss the rule and review the unit where the rule was presented.

A final comment. Rules are wonderful for cutting down on the need to memorize individual words. Sadly, the English language goes only so far in being consistent about patterns. For every rule there are exceptions that must simply be memorized. Good spellers use a variety of tactics to handle such words. Some tactics involve looking at words carefully; other tactics involve listening to the word; finally, there are those relying on memory tricks. It is important to discuss these tactics so that your child can begin using them to spell difficult words wherever they are encountered.

UNIT 21

Syllables and Stress

Dictate the Unit and Challenge Words. Say each word clearly, read the sentence, and repeat the word. For example:
animals—We saw a variety of **animals** on our camping trip.
—**animals**

Unit Words

animals	We enjoyed the **animals** in the zoo.
bottom	The **bottom** of the sea is fascinating.
discover	Prospectors dream they will **discover** gold.
equipment	Heavy **equipment** is needed for this job.
family	The **family** next door is very friendly.
finishing	I am **finishing** my homework.
hospital	The victim was rushed to the **hospital**.
machine	I wish I had a time **machine**.
police	The **police** were called to the accident.
pollution	The **pollution** index was dangerously high.
situation	Have you ever been in this **situation**?
squirrel	The **squirrel** scampered up the tree.
suddenly	The earth **suddenly** began to shake.
television	What is your favourite **television** show?
together	We enjoy playing basketball **together**.

Challenge Words
beautiful★
dinosaur
everybody
interesting
vegetable

★One of the 25 most commonly
misspelled words.

It was a **beautiful** day for hiking.
We saw a **dinosaur** exhibit at the museum.
I hope **everybody** will come to the party.
That's an **interesting** question!
We planted the **vegetable** garden in the spring.

Rewrite any misspelled words. Pay close attention to any letters that gave
you difficulty.

What's the Secret?

1. Make three columns on the page and rewrite each Unit and Challenge Word
in the correct column.

two syllables	three syllables	more than three syllables

2. Which two words could fit into more than one column, depending on how
they are pronounced?

Words that have syllables that are not pronounced make spelling more
challenging. A tactic to remember these is to pronounce the syllable when you
spell the word even if you don't say it in normal speech. For example, say
"**veg•e•ta•ble**."

3. In a word with two or more syllables, at least one of the syllables is said more
loudly, or with more stress, than the other. Dictionaries use an accent mark in
dark type following the stressed syllable, as in **ex•cept´**.

Place the accent mark after the stressed syllable in each of the following
words. Check a dictionary if you are unsure of where to place the accent.

   a) **di•no•saur**   b) **to•geth•er**   c) **ma•chine**

Spelling Secret #21

Saying words in syllables can help with spelling them.
In words of two or more syllables, one syllable is spoken with more force,
or **stress**, than the other syllables.

   For example: **oc´•to•pus**

Putting the Secret to Work

When you look up a word of more than one syllable in the dictionary, it will be
shown already divided into syllables. Each syllable is separated by a black dot.

   For example: **fre•quent•ly**

1. Print the following Unit Words as they appear in a dictionary:

   a) **pollution** b) **television**   c) **discover**

2. Unscramble these syllables to reveal Challenge Words:
- a) **ti•ful•beau**
- b) **est•ing•ter•in**
- c) **y•eve•bod•ry**
- d) **ble•veg•ta•e**

The word **squirrel** comes from the Greek word *skiouros*, meaning "shadow tail." Because a squirrel's tail is so large, it seems to become a sunshade when it is raised!

3. Complete each sentence with one of the words given. The word must have the number of syllables shown on the blank.
- a) **dinosaur   octopus   squirrel**

I drew a picture of a/an ____(2)_____ in my notebook.

- b) **television   umbrella   machine**

We bought a new ____(4)_____ when we went shopping.

4. Write the Unit and Challenge Words that have the number of syllables and the stress pattern as shown below:
- a) two syllables; stress on final syllable (2 words)
- b) three syllables; stress on second syllable (4 words)

5. Four Unit Words contain double consonants.
Double consonants can be hard to remember for spelling. Write the four words with double consonants. Try one of these tactics to remember the correct spelling:
- •print the double consonants in a different colour of ink;
- •make these letters larger than the rest;
- •use a highlighter pen to make the double consonants stand out.

Home Connections

If your child finds it difficult to hear where the stress lies in a word, it may help to "tap" out the word together. Use a light tap for unstressed syllables and a heavy tap for the stressed syllable. You can help your child to deal with longer words by writing each syllable on an index card as in the example below. Play a game of unscrambling the cards to form real words. You could begin with one word and build to the point where several words are scrambled together.

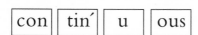

Compound Words

Dictate the Unit and Challenge Words. Say each word clearly, read the sentence, and repeat the word.

Unit Words

afternoon	The baby is having an **afternoon** nap.
anyone	Does **anyone** know who did this?
breakfast	What did you eat for **breakfast** today?
cupboard	The crackers are in the **cupboard**.
nothing	There was **nothing** left after the bake sale.
earthquake	The **earthquake** caused great damage.
everyday	It was an **everyday** occurrence.
everything	Have you remembered **everything**?
firefighter	The **firefighter** was injured on the job.
granddaughter	Her **granddaughter** came for a visit.
headache	Is your **headache** any better?
kindergarten	My sister is attending **kindergarten**.
nowhere	The car seemed to come out of **nowhere**.
something★	Are you looking for **something**?
worthwhile	That was a **worthwhile** project.

Challenge Words

bookkeeper	The **bookkeeper** kept our accounts updated.
extraordinary	It was an **extraordinary** act of courage.
hitchhike	He tried to **hitchhike** across Canada.
nighttime	At **nighttime** I like to read scary stories.
pastime	Reading is my favourite **pastime**.

★One of the 25 most commonly misspelled words.

Rewrite any misspelled words. Pay close attention to any letters that gave you difficulty.

What's the Secret?

When spelling **extraordinary**, think of **extra ordinary**.

1. Compound words are not simply little words inside a big word. There is a logical connection between the parts of a compound word.

For example: **kneepad** is a compound word; **donation** is not a compound. Which of the following words are compound words? Why?

carpet	**carwash**
carload	**carport**
cargo	**carnation**

2. Sometimes a compound word will have a double consonant in the middle because of joining the two words together.

For example: **earring = ear + ring**

An exception to this rule is the Challenge Word **pastime**, formed from **pass** and **time**.

It is easier to remember the double consonants if you think of the two words forming the compound.

Write the Unit and Challenge Words below, then separate each word as in the example above.

bookkeeper
granddaughter
hitchhike
nighttime

Spelling Secret #22

Compound words are formed from two smaller words and have a meaning related to the smaller words.

Putting the Secret to Work

1. Combine the words in the box to form compound words including some from the Unit and Challenge lists:

ground	head	fighter
ache	fire	play

2. Some compound words have interesting origins that often help us to spell the word. Match the following Unit Words with their original meanings.

a) **breakfast**   garden of children (German)
b) **kindergarten**   a shelf or board where cups are kept
c) **cupboard**   to end a fast (a time of not eating)

3. Some words are commonly joined to make many compound words. Try to form at least ten compound words by combining words in the box below. You may use the boxed words more than once.

  Not all the words will combine to form actual compounds. Check in a dictionary if you are unsure.

any	where	some	every
thing	no	one	time

4. Solve these Wacky Riddles with compound words from the Unit and Challenge Lists!

a) A nervous planet
b) Someone not welcome at a library
c) The chief pain

Draw EARTHQUAKE so that the letters are being tossed around.

5. The word **everyday** can be used as a compound word only when it modifies a noun, as in this example:

  "Laughter was an **everyday** occurrence in our family." Otherwise, "every" and "day" must be kept separate, as in "Every day my dog meets me at the bus stop."

Complete these sentences with either "everyday" or "every day."
a) Do you come here _____?
b) She wears _____ clothes to work.
c) Walking the dog was an _____ chore for Paul.
d) I try to write in my journal _____.

Home Connections

Play a game of looking for compound words related to food. Examine super-market ads, fast food coupons, magazines, and so forth, and record the compound words. Then try to guess the compound word by giving clues: e.g., a beef patty topped with cheese (cheeseburger). Or try to make up silly definitions to fit the words: e.g., What is a comedian's favourite food? (a hamburger).

UNIT 23

Adding *ed, ing, y*: Dropping the final *e*

Dictate the Unit and Challenge Words. Say each word clearly, read the sentence, and repeat the word.

Unit Words

coming	When are you **coming** home?
decided	We **decided** to go to the movies.
driving	They are **driving** to Alberta this summer.
fired	The employee was **fired** for dishonesty.
having	Are you **having** a good time?
laughed	They **laughed** at the funny story.
learned	What have you **learned** from this research?
lived	I **lived** there for three years.
removing	They are **removing** the toxins from the dump.
screamed	The child **screamed** when she lost her toy.
juicy	There was a **juicy** apple in his lunch.
watching	What program are you **watching**?
icy	The roads were very **icy** this morning.
writing	We are **writing** to our penpals in Australia.
noisy	That was a **noisy** party!

Challenge Words

exciting	The game was really **exciting**.
frightened	Were you **frightened** by the horror movie?
listened	I should have **listened** to you.
surrounded	The winning team was **surrounded** by fans.
practising	They are **practising** plays for the next game.

Rewrite any misspelled words. Pay close attention to any letters that gave you difficulty.

What's the Secret?

1. We call the part of a word we add an **ending** to the **base word.**

For example: **walk** + **ing** = **walking**

a) Write the **base word** for each of the following Unit Words:

having   driving   coming   learned   laughed   watching

b) You may have noticed in Exercise a) that half of the base words remained the same when an ending was added (learn—**learn**ed; laugh—**laugh**ed; watch—**watch**ing), while the other half dropped a letter (have—**hav**ing; drive—**driv**ing; come—**com**ing).

What letter did these base words end in?

2. Complete the following "word equations," making any needed changes to the base words.

a) **fire**   + **ed**   = _____
b) **frighten** + **ed**   = _____
c) **excite**   + **ing**   = _____
d) **listen**   + **ing**   = _____

3. Most words show something happened in the past by adding **ed** to the base word.

For example: I **remove** my wet shoes at the door.

I **removed** them when I came in.

Complete the following base words so that they show the past tense.

listen   scream   decide   practise   surround   learn

4. Some words do not show the past tense by adding **ed** to the base word.

For example: present: **come**   past: **came**

Complete this sentence with the correct past form of the base word in the box.

have   write   drive

I _____ to finish my homework, so I _____ the answers in the car while my father _____ me to school.

Spelling Secret #23

Many words are formed by adding **ed, ing,** or **y** to a base word, as in **jump, jumped, jumping.** Words ending in **ed** usually describe an event in the past.

Most words ending in **e** drop the **e** before adding the ending **ed, ing,** or **y.**

For example: **chase** + **ed** = **chased**

chase + **ing** = **chasing**

ice + **y** = **icy**

Putting the Secret to Work

1. Complete the sentences below, adding **ed**, **ing**, or **y** to the base words in the brackets.

a) It was fun __(listen)___ to the __(noise)___ birthday party next door.

b) The parents had __(decide)__ to hire a clown for the party and the children were __(laugh)___ at his silly pranks and __(watch)___ his magic tricks.

c) My brother was __(frighten)_____ by the __(scare)_____ movie.

2. In the base word **laugh**, the *f* sound at the end is spelled **gh**. A few other English words also spell *f* with the letters **gh**. Can you find them?

a) This sandpaper is very __ __ __ gh.

b) Cover your mouth when you __ __ __ gh.

c) This meat is so __ __ __ gh!

d) No, thank you. I've had __ __ __ __ gh.

Home Connections

The concept of a base or root word is extremely important, since it allows the speller to see the logical ways in which words are built.

When your child asks for help in spelling a long word, first ask what the base word is. This is different from asking, "What little words are in the big word?" For example, in the word **swearing**, the base word is **swear**, not **ear**. By helping your child to examine words logically, you are building spelling skills beyond the level of sounding words out or memorization.

UNIT 24

Adding *ed, ing, y*

Dictate the Unit and Challenge Words. Say each word clearly, read the sentence, and repeat the word.

Unit Words

stepped	I **stepped** onto the soft grass.
picked	Have we **picked** enough wildflowers?
blurred	My vision was **blurred** by the fog.
dragged	The dog **dragged** the bone away.
foggy	We had to drive in the **foggy** weather.
trimmed	The hairdresser **trimmed** her bangs.
spotted	A famous actress was **spotted** in the store.
crashing	The ball came **crashing** through the window.
knotted	The lace was hopelessly **knotted**.
combed	Have you **combed** your hair?
funny	What a **funny** story!
stopped	We **stopped** at the red light.

shrugged	She **shrugged** her shoulders and walked away.
swimming	Would you like to come **swimming** with us?
winning	The **winning** team received a trophy.

Challenge Words

knitting	I am **knitting** a sweater for my grandson.
striped	I like your **striped** shirt.
stripped	We **stripped** the old wallpaper off the wall.
scared	The sudden noise **scared** us all.
scarred	The man's face was **scarred** from the burns.

Rewrite any misspelled words. Pay close attention to any letters that gave you difficulty.

What's the Secret?

1. Write the base word for each of the following Unit and Challenge Words:

> **blurred   swimming   funny   spotted   knitting   foggy**

Look carefully at the base words. They all end with a vowel and consonant. What happens when **ed**, **ing**, or **y** are added to these words?

2. Examine these two sets of Challenge Words:

> **striped—stripped   scared—scarred**

Say each word aloud. Now write the base words. Notice what happens when **ed** is added to each base. What happens to base words ending in **e**? To base words ending in **vowel + consonant**?

Spelling Secret #24

When a one-syllable word ends in a vowel and consonant, the consonant is doubled when adding **ed**, **ing**, or **y**.

> For example: **slam + ed = slammed**
> **win + ing = winning**
> **fog + y = foggy**

Putting the Secret to Work

The rule for adding endings to words of more than one syllable, as in **transmit**, is more complex and will be dealt with in Unit 32.

1. Fill in the empty squares in the chart below:

Base	+ ed	+ ing	+ y
a) **stop**			
b) **blur**			
c) **step**			
d) **win**			
e) **fog**			

2. Complete these sentences with the following Challenge Words:

striped   stripped   scared   scarred

a) We _____ the old wallpaper off and put up new paper with a _____ pattern.

b) The farmer _____ away the fox, but the farm dog was left _____ and bruised.

3. a) In rows A, B, C, and D choose the one word that **doubles the consonant** when **ed**, **ing**, or **y** are added.

In rows E, F, G, and H choose the one word that drops an **e** when **ed**, **ing**, or **y** are added.

A	laugh	rob	stretch	watch
B	dream	listen	yap	comb
C	kiss	scream	learn	grab
D	map	frighten	roar	sound
E	reach	edge	label	scar
F	need	sleep	feed	operate
G	cream	dread	erase	allergy
H	tame	enter	finger	spell

b) Now take the first letter of the word you have chosen from each row. Use the code to answer this riddle:

Question: What is a math teacher's favourite tree?

Answer: __ __ __ __ __ __ __ __

ROW   C E F D G H A B

4. The Unit Word **combed** contains a silent *b*. The **mb** pattern is found at the end of several English words.

Combine the letters on the word wheel to form twelve other words ending in **mb**.

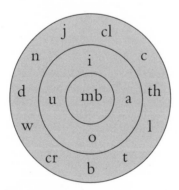

Home Connections

Encourage your child to play word games with you. There are many sources in bookstores, children's magazines, newspapers, and books. You can also have fun making up your own games.

Dictate the Unit and Challenge Words. Say each word clearly, read the sentence, and repeat the word.

Adding *ed* and *ing*

Unit Words

tried	Have you **tried** doing it this way?
buried	The nuts were **buried** by the squirrel.
copied	I **copied** the information onto the sheet.
cried	We **cried** at the end of the movie.
denying	I am not **denying** you were right.
funniest	That was the **funniest** joke of the night!
glorious	It was a **glorious** sunset.
happiness	Her smile showed her **happiness**.
loneliness	He complained of **loneliness** while at camp.
occupied	All the seats are **occupied**.
qualified	Is the lifeguard **qualified**?
studying	When are you **studying** for the test?
supplied	We were **supplied** with warm clothes.
various	There are **various** types of carrot seeds.
worried	You seem **worried** about something.

Challenge Words

classified	The ad appeared in the **classified** section.
friendliness	Everyone enjoys his **friendliness**.
hurried	I **hurried** to school after I missed the bus.
married	How long have they been **married**?
mysterious	There was a **mysterious** stranger in the novel.

Rewrite any misspelled words. Pay close attention to any letters that gave you difficulty.

What's the Secret?

1. Study the following chart. Each base word ends with a **consonant** + **y**.

    a) What happens to the base word when **ing** is added to these base words?

    b) What happens to the base word when endings other than **ing** are added?

Base	+ ing	+ ed	+ est
bury	burying	buried	
copy	copying	copied	
funny			funniest

2. Three of the Unit and Challenge Words end in **ous**. Write these words and their base words. Notice that the **y** at the end of the base word changes to **i** when **ous** is added.

> ### Spelling Secret #25
> When a base word ends in a **consonant** + **y**, as in **cry**, keep the final **y** when adding **ing**.
>   For example: **cry** + **ing** = **crying**
>   When adding endings other than **ing,** change the **y** to **i**.
>   For example: **apply** + **ed** = **applied**
>   **happy** + **ness** = **happiness**
>   **mystery** + **ous** = **mysterious**

Putting the Secret to Work

1. Complete the following Classified Ads and News Bulletins by following the directions in brackets:

Classified Ads

a) Hire Giggles the Clown for your (**funny** + **est**) birthday ever!

b) Fully (**qualify** + **ed**) swimming instructor. References (**supply** + **ed**) on request.

c) Are you (**worry** + **ing**) about your vacation? Spend two (**glory** + **ous**) weeks in Prince Edward Island. (**Friend** + **ly** + **ness**) guaranteed!

News Flash!

d) (**Mystery** + **ous**) fire breaks out in apartment building. Children playing nearby (**deny** + **ing**) responsibility.

e) Skiers (**bury** + **ed**) in avalanche. Rescuers (**try** + **ed**) to dig them out. (**Worry** + **ed**) friends rejoice when skiers are found!

2. Add **ous** to each of the base words below.

Notice how the pronunciation of *study* changes when **ous** is added to make *studious*.

3. Eight of the Unit and Challenge Words contain double consonants. It is important to remember these consonants when spelling the words. Write each Unit and Challenge Word containing a double consonant. Use a tactic to make these letters stand out in your mind. (Circle them; write them in a different colour; or use a highlighter pen.)

4. A base word such as **classify** can be expanded to form a number of related words:

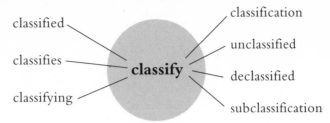

classified

classifies

classifying

classify

classification

unclassified

declassified

subclassification

5. Build as many words as you can from the base word **friend**. Use a dictionary to help.

Home Connections

Look through newspapers and magazines for words that end in **ing** or **ed**. Make a list of these words. Then write the base word for each. Sort them into two categories—those in which no changes were made to the base word and those in which a letter in the base word was dropped, added, etc.

For example:

No Change	Change
award—awarded	celebrate—celebrated
defeat—defeated	promise—promised
report—reporting	get—getting
carry—carrying	marry—married

UNIT 26

Dictate the Unit and Challenge Words. Say each word clearly, read the sentence, and repeat the word.

Adding *ly*

Unit Words

carefully	Place your projects **carefully** on the shelf.
certainly	I am **certainly** going to remember this day!
continually	The child was **continually** fussing.
surely	You must **surely** be joking!
happily	We returned home **happily** after our busy day.
apparently	**Apparently** the test was cancelled.
lonely	Were you **lonely** at camp?
lovely	There was a **lovely** sunset last evening.
probably	There are **probably** five different solutions.
quickly	How **quickly** can you get here?
quietly	Please play **quietly** in your room.
angrily	The woman reacted **angrily** to the news.
steadily	The lava flowed **steadily** down the mountainside.
terribly	I'm **terribly** sorry I hurt you.
awfully	We were **awfully** cold on the long hike.

Challenge Words

actually
truly
definitely
incredibly
finally

I was **actually** planning to go shopping today.
He was **truly** sorry for making the remark.
You will **definitely** be receiving an invitation.
That stunt is **incredibly** difficult to do.
I think I can **finally** fall asleep now.

Rewrite any misspelled words. Pay close attention to any letters that gave you difficulty.

What's the Secret?

1. Write the base words for the following Unit and Challenge Words:

carefully   awfully   finally   continually   actually

Notice that the double consonants **ll** in the words above are formed when **ly** is added to the base word, which ends in **l**.

In the word **definitely** *look for the word* **finite**.

2. When **ly** is added to words ending in silent *e*, such as **love**ly, **lone**ly, and **definite**ly, no change is made to the base word.

Add **ly** to the following words:

sure	active	polite
rare	loose	entire
close	like	live

Remember to say **probably** *clearly so that you hear the second* **b**.

3. Notice what happens when **ly** is added to words ending in **le**, such as:

probable—probably   incredible—incredibly

Complete each "word equation" below:

terrible + **ly**   = _____
horrible + **ly**   = _____
responsible + **ly**   = _____
comfortable + **ly** = _____
fashionable + **ly** = _____

Exception: An exception to the pattern above is the word **truly**, where the silent *e* is dropped from the base word **true** when **ly** is added.

4. Write the base words for the following Unit Words:

angrily   happily   steadily

What happens to the base word when **ly** is added?

Spelling Secret #26

The ending **ly** is added to many words. For example:
friend + **ly** = **friendly**   **lone** + **ly** = **lonely**
When adding **ly** to words ending in **le**, as in **terrible**, drop the **le**. For example: **terrible** + **ly** = **terribly**
When adding **ly** to words ending in **y**, as in **heavy**, change the **y** to **i**.
For example: **heavy** + **ly** = **heavily**

Putting the Secret to Work

1. Complete the following sentences by adding **ly** to the words in brackets:

a) The children were (**busy**) playing in the sand while their parents lounged (**lazy**) in their chairs.

b) I can (**easy**) finish cutting the lawn in an hour. (**Lucky**) I have a new power mower.

c) The puppies yapped (**noisy**) as they crawled (**clumsy**) over their mother. Soon they were quiet as they (**hungry**) drank her milk.

2. Complete the puzzle with Unit and Challenge Words.

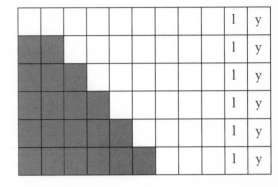

a) constantly; without interruption

b) surely; no doubt

c) most likely; a good chance

d) with little noise

e) feeling alone

f) Yours _____,

3. a) How many words do you know that begin with the letters **qu**? After you have used up your own ideas, check in the dictionary.

b) Does your dictionary list any English words that begin with **q**, but are <u>not</u> followed by **u**?

Home Connections

"Tom Swifties" are jokes that use **adverbs** to create puns. Once you start this game it's difficult to stop! Here are some examples of "Tom Swifties":

"Is the doctor here yet?" he asked patiently.

"Drop that knife!" he said sharply.

"I'd prefer a hot dog," she replied frankly.

"You erased the whole file!" he muttered blankly.

UNIT 27

Plurals

Dictate the Unit and Challenge Words. Say each word clearly, read the sentence, and repeat the word.

Unit Words

actresses   The **actresses** studied their parts.

addresses   The **addresses** of the students are here.

guesses   How many **guesses** are we allowed?

heroes   The **heroes** all received medals.

illnesses   We suffered from a variety of **illnesses**.

mailboxes	The **mailboxes** were filled with letters.
pianos	The piano tuner tuned three **pianos**.
pictures	The **pictures** were pinned to the board.
radios	How many **radios** do you have at home?
scratches	The **scratches** were very painful.
skis	Be sure to wax your **skis** properly.
speeches	We listened to the **speeches** on the radio.
tomatoes	The **tomatoes** are growing in the garden.
toothbrushes	We packed our **toothbrushes** in the case.
videos	We watched three **videos** yesterday.

Challenge Words

businesses	Several **businesses** donated prizes.
circuses	I saw three **circuses** on my trip.
languages	How many **languages** can you speak?
mosquitoes	The **mosquitoes** were very annoying.
sandwiches	We have egg, ham, and cheese **sandwiches**.

Rewrite any misspelled words. Pay close attention to any letters that gave you difficulty.

What's the Secret?

1. Write the following Unit Words. Beside each write the singular form.

For example: **actresses—actress**

circuses   guesses   toothbrushes   speeches   mailboxes

How is the plural formed in words ending in **s**, **ss**, **sh**, **ch**, and **x**?

2. There is no simple rule for making words ending in **o** plural. In most cases, **s** is added, as in photo—photo**s**.

There are many cases, however, when the letters **es** are added, as in **potato—potatoes**.

A handy rule is that if a word ending in **o** is related to the topic of **music**, form the plural by adding **s**.

For example: **banjos**

Write the plural form of the following Unit and Challenge Words.

| **hero** | **radio** | **mosquito** |
| **piano** | **video** | **tomato** |

Spelling Secret #27

To form the plural of most words add **s**.

For example: girl**s**

To form the plural of words ending with **s**, **ss**, **sh**, **ch**, and **x** add **es**.

For example: bus**es**, dress**es**, bush**es**, church**es**, box**es**

Putting the Secret to Work

1. Form the plural of each word on the word pole below:

S EARCH
A STRONAUT
N OSE
D ISH
W AX
I GUANA
C AMPUS
H OAX
E CHO
S OPRANO

2. Complete each set of words with a Unit or Challenge Word.
  a) **beans**; **carrots**; **squash**; _____
  b) **moths**; **houseflies**; **bees**; _____
  c) **combs**; **mirrors**; **towels**; _____
  d) **toboggans**; **skates**; **sleighs**; _____
  e) **guitars**; **drums**; **violins**; _____

3. Some of the Unit and Challenge Words have letters that are not clearly heard when you say the words aloud.
  a) Complete each of the words below:

g__esses	bus__nesses	scra__ches
pi__tures	lang__ages	c__rcuses
san__wiches	a__ __ resses	i__ __ nesses

4. In ancient Rome the word **circus** referred to a "ring." How does the modern-day circus fit this definition?

Home Connections

Watch the newspapers, flyers, and so forth for examples of the plural forms of words. It is important for your child to develop a mental image of plurals such as potato**es**, sk**is**, etc.

UNIT 28

Plurals

Unit Words

allergies   My **allergies** make my face puff out.
beliefs   Each culture has its own set of **beliefs**.
biographies   I enjoy reading **biographies** of famous people.
calves   There are three **calves** in the barn.

centuries	The crusades took place **centuries** ago.
children	The **children** played on the equipment.
deer	The **deer** were killed by poachers.
enemies	We tried to make peace with our **enemies**.
journeys	My **journeys** are recorded in my diary.
people	How many **people** were at the party?
sheriffs	The **sheriffs** wore their badges proudly.
themselves	They repaired the bikes by **themselves**.
valleys	The green **valleys** were beautiful.
wolves	The hungry **wolves** fought over the dead rabbit.
women	How many **women** are in your family?

Challenge Words

dictionaries	The **dictionaries** are on the front shelf.
giraffes	The **giraffes** nibbled on the tall trees.
knives	The **knives** were stuck in the butcher's block.
libraries	I called several **libraries** about the book.
luxuries	Bath oils and fancy soaps are **luxuries**.

Rewrite any misspelled words. Pay close attention to any letters that gave you difficulty.

What's the Secret?

1. Look carefully at the words in columns A and B:

A	B
valley	allergy
journey	enemy
turkey	luxury

What is the key difference between the words in columns A and B?
Now notice the plural forms of these words:

A	B
valleys	allergies
journeys	enemies
turkeys	luxuries

How do the plural forms differ in the two sets of words?

2. Most words that end in **f** or **fe** form the plural by adding **s**.
   For example, chief—chief**s**.
There are some exceptions to this rule, as shown below:

calf	calves	loaf	loaves
elf	elves	self	selves
half	halves	shelf	shelves
knife	knives	thief	thieves
leaf	leaves	wife	wives
life	lives	wolf	wolves

3. Some plurals are not formed in the usual ways and must simply be memorized. A list of some of these forms is below:

child	**children**
man	**men**
woman	**women**
deer	**deer**
person	**people**

Spelling Secret #28

To form the plural of words ending in a **vowel + y**, as in **turkey**, add **s**.

> For example: turkey—turkey**s**

To form the plural of words ending in a **consonant** plus **y**, as in **country**, change the **y** to **i** and add **es**.

> For example: country—countr**ies**

To form the plural of words ending in **f** or **fe**, as in **chief** or **giraffe**, add **s**. (there are exceptions)

> For example: chief—chief**s**   giraffe—giraffe**s**

Putting the Secret to Work

1. The following sentences contain words that end in a **vowel + y** and others that end in a **consonant + y**.

Complete each sentence with the plural form of the words in brackets:

a) We saw the (**monkey**) and their (**baby**) at the petting zoo.

b) (**Survey**) have shown that regular brushing can prevent (**cavity**).

c) Our (**journey**) have taken us to twenty-one (**country**).

2. The plural form of most nouns can be found by looking at a dictionary entry for the singular form of the word.

> For example, the dictionary entry for the word **shelf** has the plural spelling after the singular.

> **Shelf** (shelf) *n., pl.* **shelves. 1** a thin, flat piece of wood, or other material, fastened to a wall or frame to hold things, such as books, dishes, etc. **2** anything like a shelf.

Look in a dictionary for the spelling of the plural form of the following words. These words have unusual plurals because they have kept their original Latin form.

a) **diagnosis**   b) **hypothesis**   c) **datum**

Remember to say the **r** in **library**

3. Words that have silent letters, such as **calf** and **knife**, or double consonants, as in **giraffe** and **sheriff**, are tricky to spell. Sounding the word out won't help, so you need tactics that will help you to remember the word by **sight**.

Configuration: this tactic involves remembering the **shape** of the word. It is especially good for silent or double consonants.

For example: **valley**

Match the words in column A with shapes in column B:

	A		B
a)	sheriff	1.	
b)	calf	2.	
c)	knife	3.	
d)	giraffe	4.	
e)	allergy	5.	

Centipede is formed from the Latin *centum* (hundred) and *pes, pedis* (foot).

4. "Cent" comes from the Latin word *centum*, meaning "hundred." How do the following words make sense using this definition? If you are not sure, consult your dictionary.

    a) **century**
    b) **cent**
    c) **bicentennial**
    d) **centimetre**

Home Connections

Try playing the following word-building game with your child:

How many words can you write about **FOOD**, using only the letters below? (A letter can be used more than once in the same word.)

Add an **s** or **es** to all the words you can. Give yourself a point for each letter you use.

    For example: **potato** = **6** points
                  potatoes = **8** points
                  Total = **14** points

a b p i c n f h d u e r y k s l o t

0 to 100 points: just a nibble!
101 to 150 points: getting full?
151 to 200 points: what an appetite!

Possessives

The possessive form of a noun shows ownership.

Dictate the Unit and Challenge Words. Say each word clearly, read the sentence, and repeat the word.

Unit Words

atlas's	This **atlas's** maps are out-of-date.
authors'	The two **authors'** books are on display.
babies'	Several **babies'** diapers were folded neatly.
bridge's	The **bridge's** main support was damaged.
children's	The **children's** games were very popular.
computer's	The **computer's** hard drive was being fixed.
customers'	The three **customers'** complaints were recorded.
editor's	I followed my **editor's** suggestion for the book.
goalie's	The **goalie's** pads stopped the hard puck.
horses'	The **horses'** manes were beautifully groomed.
house's	The **house's** address was difficult to see.
judges'	The two **judges'** decisions were final.
nurse's	The **nurse's** back was hurt lifting a patient.
passengers'	We waited in the **passengers'** lounge.
school's	The **school's** flag was lowered to half mast.

Challenge Words

cousin's	My **cousin's** bike was stolen on the weekend.
government's	The **government's** new policy was presented.
guitar's	The **guitar's** string broke during the concert.
league's	She is the **league's** most valuable player.
referees'	The **referees'** uniforms are over there.

Rewrite any misspelled words. Pay close attention to any letters that gave you difficulty.

What's the Secret?

1. When we say, "The boy's shirts," we mean "the shirts belonging to the boy." If we are talking about only one boy, we simply add apostrophe (') and **s**.
The same rule applies when a singular noun ends in **s**, as in **boss**.
   "the boss**'s** orders were quickly obeyed."
Complete the following phrases with the possessive form.
   a) the mask belonging to the goalie   the _____ mask
   b) the hem of the dress   the _____ hem
   c) the comments of the editor   the _____ comments
   d) the mascot for the school   the _____ mascot

2. Look at the example in Exercise 1. If we were talking about the shirts of **more than one boy**, we would simply add an apostrophe to the plural form.

For example: The boy**s'** shirts—the shirts belonging to the boys.

The buse**s'** parking lot—the parking lot for the buses.

Rewrite each phrase from Exercise 1 so that the plural form is made possessive.

a) the masks belonging to the goalies the _____ masks

b) the hems of the dresses the _____ hems

c) the comments of the editors the _____ comments

d) the mascots for the schools the _____ mascots

3. The special plural forms described in Unit 28 form the possessive by adding **'s**. For example: the children**'s** coats. Write the possessive form for each word below:

a) **men**: the _____ locker room

b) **women**: the _____ basketball team

c) **people**: the _____ choice

Spelling Secret #29

The **possessive** form of a noun shows ownership.

When a noun is singular, as in **girl** or **bus**, add apostrophe (') and **s**.

For example: the **girl's** shirt, the **bus's** wheels

When a plural noun already ends in **s**, as in **players**, add just an apostrophe ('). For example: the **players'** uniforms

For plural nouns, such as **children**, add apostrophe (') and **s**.

For example: the **children's** playground

Putting the Secret to Work

1. Many people confuse the plural and possessive forms, since both have an **s** at the end. Choose either the plural or possessive form of the word in brackets that fits the sentence.

a) (**Houses, House's**) of all sizes were advertised in the newspaper.

b) My (**guitars, guitar's**) strings were broken by my young (**cousins, cousin's**).

c) The (**babies, babies'**) blankets were folded neatly by their (**parents, parents'**).

2. Choose words from each column of the chart to form possessive phrases, then write the possessive form. Mix and match words from different rows and see how many phrases you can come up with!

For example: the **women's** opinions

a) The	bicycles	of the	men
b) The	racquets	of the	women
c) The	opinions	of the	people
d) The	antlers	of the	deer

3. Notice how the sound *g* is spelled in the Challenge Words **guitar's** and **league's**. Complete the puzzle below with words containing **gu**.

a) **gu** __ __ __ __ opposite of innocent
b) **f** __ __ __ **gu** __ weariness; tiredness
c) **gu** __ __ __ to show the way
d) __ __ __ **gu** __ part of the mouth
e) **d** __ __ **gu** __ __ __ costume; hide identity

Home Connections

Make a habit of watching for misspelled plural and possessive forms in your community—store signs, advertising flyers, newspapers. There is a recent trend toward adding 's to a singular word and assuming it is plural!

For example: "**Tomato's for sale**"

Encourage your child to look for such errors; decide what the correct spelling should be.

UNIT 30

A **contraction** is a shortened form of two words.

Dictate the Unit and Challenge Words. Say each word clearly, read the sentence, and repeat the word.

Contractions

Unit Words

didn't★	I **didn't** go outside for recess.
wasn't	He **wasn't** ready for school in the morning.
what's	Do you know **what's** for dinner tonight?
there's★	I think **there's** too much fighting.
I'm	**I'm** ready to go out now.
you're	We know **you're** in there!
its	The dog hurt **its** tail in the door.
it's★	Are you sure **it's** all right to come in?
let's★	It's really hot, so **let's** go swimming.
that's★	I think **that's** a really good idea.
they've	I can tell **they've** been here.
we'd	Do you think **we'd** better leave?
don't	Why **don't** you like this sweater?
wouldn't	The child **wouldn't** go near the large dog.
we're	Today **we're** leaving for Yellowknife.

Challenge Words

doesn't	The hamster **doesn't** like to be held.
it'll	My mom says **it'll** be cold today.
they're	Tomorrow **they're** going to the movies.
weren't	We **weren't** allowed to go to the party.
can't	I **can't** throw a curve ball.

Rewrite any misspelled words. Pay close attention to any letters that gave you difficulty.

What's the Secret?

1. Contractions may be formed by removing one or more letters from the original two words.

> For example: **you are—you're** (one letter removed)
>
> **I would—I'd** (four letters removed)

Sort the Unit and Challenge Words into two columns, as in the chart below:

one letter removed	more than one letter removed
you are–you're	I would–I'd

Spelling Secret #30

A contraction is a shortened form of two words. One or more letters are removed and replaced by an apostrophe, as in **you are—you're**.

Putting the Secret to Work

1. Write contractions for the words in bold in the following sentences.

a) **We would** like to borrow that tape but **they have** already signed it out.

b) **Here is** a picture of my kindergarten class. I **do not** recognize many of the children because **we have** all changed so much.

c) It **does not** matter if **you are** six or sixty—you **will not** be disappointed by this movie.

2. Many question words make contractions with the word **is**.

> For example: **where is—where's**

Rewrite these questions by substituting contractions for the words in bold:

a) **Who is** going to the game today?

b) **When is** it being played?

c) **What is** the admission price?

d) **How is** the weather?

3. Form contractions by combining words from columns A and B, or B and C. From your list of contractions, choose four to use in sentences.

> For example: **they + would = they'd**
>
> They said **they'd** be here by noon.

A	B	C
they	has	not
she	is	
I	have	
he	are	
you	am	
	should	
	could	
	would	
	does	

Remember, if you can substitute the phrase "it is" in the sentence, use the contraction **it's**.

4. Many people confuse the possessive **its**, as in, "The dog was wagging **its** tail," with the contraction **it's**, as in "**It's** a beautiful day!"

Use the correct form of **its/it's** in the following sentences.

a) **Its/It's** interesting to watch a spider building **its/it's** web.

b) If **its/it's** not too much trouble, would you return the book to **its/it's** proper shelf?

c) When the squirrel stuffs **its/it's** cheeks with nuts, we know **its/it's** a sign of autumn.

If you can substitute the phrase "you are" in the sentence, use **you're**.

5. Notice the difference in meaning between the possessive form of "you"—**your** and the contraction **you're**.

For example: Are you enjoying **your** holiday? I'm glad **you're** here.

Complete the following sentences with either **you're** or **your**.

a) Are you sure _____ ready? _____ books are still on the table.

b) I really enjoy _____ sense of humour. _____ a real comedian!

Home Connections

If your child continues to have problems remembering where to place the apostrophe in a contraction, try this approach. Think of a contraction as two words that have been squeezed together very hard. The pressure is so great that one of the letters pops up and flies above the word. A piece of that letter becomes the apostrophe. That letter is usually not sounded in the contraction. For example, in "wouldn't" the "o" in "not" has popped out and can no longer be heard. A part of the "o" becomes the apostrophe. This image doesn't work for all contractions, but it does in most cases.

U N I T 3 1

Homonyms

Words that sound the same but have different spellings and meanings are called **homonyms**.

Dictate the Unit and Challenge Words. Say each word clearly, read the sentences, and repeat the word.

Unit Words

allowed	I am not **allowed** to go out tonight.
aloud	The student spoke **aloud** in class.
flour	We used cake and pastry **flour** in the cupcakes.
flower	The **flower** wilted in the heat.
passed	I **passed** the puck to my teammate.
past	We can learn a lot from the **past**.
pause	I put the video game on **pause**.
paws	My cat licked her **paws** clean.
scene	We had to practise the **scene** again.
seen	Have you **seen** my brother yet?

threw	I **threw** the baseball into the field.
through	We went **through** the park on the way home.
waist	The belt won't go around my **waist**.
waste	Don't **waste** your food.

Challenge Words

lead	I have lots of **lead** in my pencil.
led	She **led** her dog to the school for a walk.
principal	Do you know the **principal** of the school?
principle	On what **principle** does that machine operate?
who's	The lady wonders **who's** there.
whose	I wonder **whose** purse this is.

Rewrite any misspelled words. Pay close attention to any letters that gave you difficulty.

What's the Secret?

1. Read the following sentence aloud:

"I only paid a **cent** for that bottle of **scent** that I **sent** to my aunt."

The three words that sound alike in this sentence are called **homonyms**. Although they sound the same, they have different meanings and are spelled differently.

Complete each sentence with the correct homonym.

a) We saw the kitten (**pause/paws**) as she (**past/passed**) the doorway. Suddenly she (**through/threw**) herself at a ball of wool she had (**scene/seen**) on the chair.

b) Our family studies teacher never (**allowed/aloud**) us to (**waist/waste**) (**flower/flour**) when we were baking.

c) The (**principle/principal**) wanted to know (**whose/who's**) (**led/lead**) pencil was stuck in the lock.

Spelling Secret #31

Homonyms are words that sound the same but have different meanings and spellings. For example: **rode/road**

Putting the Secret to Work

1. Here are some new homonyms!

Correct the following advertisements by using the proper homonyms. Use your dictionary if you are unsure.

a) Bird cages on special—very cheep!

b) Fresh honey—our quality can't bee topped!

c) Assorted gums—you chews

d) Chocolate sundaes prepared while you weight

e) Midsummer sail—all beachwear reduced

2. Correct the homonym errors in the paragraph below:

The **passed** few **ours** have been a complete **waist** of time. I wasn't **aloud** to go to Shane's until I weeded the **flour** beds. Then my dog walked **threw** the house with mud all over his **pause**. I had never **scene** such a mess! I **lead** him out to his doghouse, and **whose their**? My little brother playing in the same mud puddle!

3. Sometimes it helps to use memory tricks to sort out homonym pairs. Here are some examples:

hear/here: Remember that you h**ear** with your **ear**!
principle/principal: Remember that the princi**pal** is your **pal**!

Try to develop some tactics for remembering the homonyms in the Unit and Challenge Lists.

4. The answer to each riddle below is a pair of homonyms. For example: I consumed one more than seven. I **ate eight**.

a) a shaved grizzly
b) a piece of lumber with nothing to do
c) a reasonable price for a bus ticket
d) an underaged worker in a mine
e) a bunny's fur
f) writing paper that is never moved

Home Connections

Try to make up more homonym riddles with your child. A good source of these riddles is the book *Hey, Hay! A Wagonful of Funny Homonym Riddles* (see Recommended Resources on page 157).

Help your child to complete this puzzle.

There are at least 20 homonyms in the puzzle below. 15 are from the Unit and Challenge Lists. See how many you can find. Start at any letter and move in any direction, but don't skip over letters.

For example: **scene/seen**

t	h	i	w	e	o
e	s	a	d	p	s
a	c	e	a	s	a
f	l	n	e	t	w
l	o	w	r	h	u
d	e	u	d	o	g

Syllables and Stress
Doubling Final Consonants

Dictate the Unit and Challenge Words. Say each word clearly, read the sentence, and repeat the word.

Unit Words

everywhere	There seem to be squirrels **everywhere**.
reasoning	This problem requires careful **reasoning**.
limited	The tickets are **limited** to two per customer.
magazine	What **magazine** are you reading?
started	Have you **started** your book report?
equipped	My CD player is **equipped** with headphones.
beginning	We went swimming at the **beginning** of summer.
admitted	I **admitted** that I'd broken the window.
opportunity	What a wonderful **opportunity**!
forgetting	He's always **forgetting** to bring his homework.
wanted	We really **wanted** to go to the theatre.
successful	Canada was very **successful** in the Olympics.
temperature	The **temperature** of the air was below zero.
occurred	The accident **occurred** after school.
transmitted	The ship **transmitted** a signal to shore.

Challenge Words

especially	I **especially** love riding Arabian horses.
immediately	She ate the ice cream **immediately**.
multiplication	Are you studying your **multiplication** tables?
necessary	That noise isn't **necessary**.
environment	That law is meant to protect the **environment**.

Rewrite any misspelled words. Pay close attention to any letters that gave you difficulty.

What's the Secret?

1. Read these words aloud: **reason limit happen**
Which syllable is stressed in these words?

What happens to the base word when **ed** and **ing** are added to this set of words?

reasoned	limited	happened
reasoning	limiting	happening

a) Add **ed** and **ing** to the following words:

pardon	listen	profit

2. Read these words aloud: **equip admit occur**

Which syllable is stressed in these words?

What happens when **ed** and **ing** are added to this set of words?

equipped	**admitted**	**occurred**
equipping	**admitting**	**occurring**

a) Add **ed** and **ing** to the following words:

expel	**transmit**	**control**

Spelling Secret #32

Recall from Unit 24 that the final consonant is doubled when **ed** and **ing** are added to one-syllable words such as **slam**. For example: slam—slam**med**

With two-syllable words ending in a vowel and consonant, whether to double the consonant depends on which syllable is **stressed**. If the stress is on the **first** syllable, as in **happen**, just add **ed** or **ing**. For example: happen—happen**ed**, happen**ing**. If the stress is on the **second** syllable, as in **permit**, double the final consonant when adding **ed** or **ing**. example: permit—permit**ted**, permit**ting**

American spelling follows the above rules closely. In some British and Canadian spellings, however, there is a tendency to double the final consonant even when the stress is on the first syllable. In the examples below, both spellings are considered acceptable, although the **first one** is usually the most often used.

Base	ed	ing
label	labelled (labeled)	labelling (labeling)
travel	travelled (traveled)	travelling (traveling)
shovel	shovelled (shoveled)	shovelling (shoveling)
cancel	cancelled (canceled)	cancelling (canceling)
equal	equalled (equaled)	equalling (equaling)
model	modelled (modeled)	modelling (modeling)

Putting the Secret to Work

1. Complete the following sentences by adding **ed** or **ing** to the words in brackets.

a) Aren't you (**forget** + **ing**) something?

b) A fresh layer of snow (**blanket** + **ed**) the ground.

c) This is just the (**begin** + **ing**) !

d) The robbers (**commit** + **ed**) a serious crime.

e) That shows logical (**reason** + **ing**).

2. Unscramble these syllables to reveal Unit and Challenge Words:

a) **por•ni•tu•op•ty**

b) **pli•tion•ca•mul•ti**

c) **es•y•sar•nec**

d) **at•tem•ure•per**

e) **ate•me•ly•di•im**

3. Many of the Unit and Challenge Words have special spelling challenges.
a) Write the **five** words that have double consonants in the **base word** (not as a result of adding an ending). Highlight the double consonants in some way: with a highlighter pen, by writing them in a different colour or in big letters.
b) Say the words **environment** and **temperature** clearly so that each letter and syllable is pronounced.
c) Think of a way to remember the spelling of the *s* sounds in ne**cess**ary.
d) What is the base word of **especially**? It should help you to spell this word.

Home Connections

Many spelling features such as double consonants in the middle of words can best be remembered by forming a "picture in the brain" of the word.

Encourage your child's **visual memory** in this way. "Pretend you are watching a television screen. Look at the picture you see. Now wipe the screen clean. Put this word on your screen (e.g., **necessary**). Notice each letter. Say each letter out loud. Now wipe off the screen. Write the word. If you have any difficulty, put the word on your mind's screen again and repeat the process."

UNIT 33

Vowels in Unstressed Syllables

Dictate the Unit and Challenge Words. Say each word clearly, read the sentence, and repeat the word.

Unit Words

bargain	My new jeans were a real **bargain**.
capital	Canberra is the **capital** of Australia.
college	Which **college** do you plan to attend?
compliment	Thank you for the **compliment**!
little	I loved that book when I was **little**.
accident	He broke his mother's vase by **accident**.
elevator	We pressed several buttons on the **elevator**.
furniture	We need new livingroom **furniture**.
horrible	She felt **horrible** about breaking the chair.
lettuce	I like **lettuce** on my sandwiches.
mountain	He took a chairlift up the **mountain**.
engine	I hope the **engine** doesn't stall.
pleasant	The weather was **pleasant** in Victoria.
possible	It's **possible** to build a better car.
minute	I will be there in a **minute**.

Challenge Words

banquet
curiosity
guarantee
nuisance
recommend

We had a great time at the sports **banquet**.
You'll have to control your **curiosity**.
I **guarantee** a fair price on this television.
My sister can be a real **nuisance**.
I **recommend** this brand as the best.

Rewrite any misspelled words. Pay close attention to any letters that gave you difficulty.

What's the Secret?

In many words, the vowels in unstressed syllables are difficult to hear. For example, the bold letters in the following words sound basically the same:

definition   repetition   opposition

1. Complete the words below with the correct vowels in the unstressed syllables.

coll__ge   cap__t__l
min__te   lett__ce
pleas__nt   eng__ne

Remember the **ea** in pl**ea**sant by thinking of pl**ea**se. You may wish to circle these letters or write them in a different colour to "fix" them in your memory.

2. Dictionaries use a special symbol to represent the pronunciation of vowels in unstressed syllables. This symbol (ə) is also known as a "schwa."

The odd-looking words below are the symbols used in the dictionary to show the pronunciation of various Unit or Challenge Words. Notice the schwa sign in each word.

Write the Unit or Challenge Word for each set of pronunciation symbols.

a) **rēk'ə mend'**
b) **kom'plə mə nt**
c) **hôr'ə bəl**
d) **gar'ən tē'**

Spelling Secret #33

The vowel sound in many unstressed syllables is difficult to hear, as in the second syllable of **lemon** or **pencil**. Pay special attention when learning to spell such words.

Putting the Secret to Work

1. Some unstressed endings can be remembered by linking them with other words with the same pattern.

Complete the word puzzle below with words ending in **ain**.

a) ___ ___ ___ ___ **ain**   a good deal
       1   2

b) ___ ___ ___ ___ **ain**   a sure thing
      3   4   5

c) ___ ___ ___ ___ **ain**   covering for windows
         6

d) ___ ___ ___ ___ **ain**   scoundrel; evil person
      7   8   9

e) ___ ___ ___ ___ **ain**   commander of a ship

f) ___ ___ ___ ___ ___ **ain**   a very high hill
     10   11   12

g) ___ ___ ___ ___ ___ **ain**   spurts water

2. Use the number code beneath the answers above to name four Canadian cities.

a) ___ ___ ___ ___ ___ ___ ___ ___ ___
     7   1   12   3   11   6   7   4   2

b) ___ ___ ___ ___ ___ ___ ___
     5   11   2   11   12   5   11

c) ___ ___ ___ ___ ___ ___ ___ ___
     10   11   12   5   2   4   1   9

d) ___ ___ ___ ___ ___ ___ ___ ___
     7   8   3   5   11   2   8   1

3. a) Circle or underline the unusual vowel combinations in the following words:
   banquet   nuisance   guarantee

b) Circle or underline the double consonants in the words below:
   college   horrible   possible   lettuce   recommend   accident

Home Connections

Another way of remembering tricky parts of words is to create memory tricks or "mnemonics." For example, remember the **ie** (not **ei**) combination in "friend" by saying, "A friend is a fri**end** to the **end**."

The best mnemonics (pronounced ni-mon-iks) are those your child creates with you. Keep a page in the spelling notebook for mnemonics the two of you create. Add to it whenever a word gives your child particular difficulty.

5 Meaning Connections

Meaning Connections

Introduction

If you have an understanding of the patterns presented in Sections 1, 2, 3, and 4 of *Sharing the Secrets*, you will likely be a fairly good speller already. You will be able to sound words out, and to apply many important spelling rules. To be a first-rate speller, however, there are a number of spelling skills you will still need to develop. The tactics you have learned for dealing with tricky words will have to be expanded and applied to a variety of challenging words. You will also need to understand how very long words are often the result of prefixes and suffixes being added to a base word. Being able to see the logic of how long words, such as "international" or "unrealistic" are constructed will also help you in your reading and level of vocabulary.

The four units in Section 5 of this book will demonstrate how words are often related in both meaning and spelling, how a knowledge of prefixes and suffixes can provide clues to spelling, and how knowing the origin of a word can lead to understanding its spelling.

Further examples of words that fit each pattern are provided in Appendix II.

UNIT 34

Related Words

Dictate the Unit and Challenge Words. Say each word clearly, read the sentence, and repeat the word.

Unit Words

competitor	I met a strong **competitor** in hockey.
confident	We were **confident** that our team would win.
criticism	There was **criticism** of the judging.
editorial	The **editorial** in the paper was very good.
excellent	The rides at the park were **excellent**.
ignorant	We were **ignorant** of the fact he was here.
invitation	I received an **invitation** to the party.
magician	They were watching the **magician** do a trick.
muscular	He had a very **muscular** build.
original	I have an **original** idea for a science project.
photography	I'm studying **photography** at night.
provincial	There will be a **provincial** election soon.
responsible	Who is **responsible** for these animals?
telescopic	There is a **telescopic** device in the museum.
going	Are you **going** to the library tonight?

Challenge Words

argument
courageous
disappearance
independent
prehistoric

Remember to drop the final **e** when going from **argue** to **argument**. Remember the double **l** when going from **excel** to **excellent**.

I had an **argument** with my parents.
The rescuer was incredibly **courageous**.
The **disappearance** of the file was puzzling.
This is an **independent** project, not group work.
They discovered a **prehistoric** fossil.

Rewrite any misspelled words. Pay close attention to any letters that gave you difficulty.

What's the Secret?

1. Long words often seem difficult to read and spell, but are actually just base words with *prefixes* (a syllable added to the beginning of a word) and *suffixes* (a syllable added to the end of a word) added. If you know how the base word is spelled, you will often have a good start in spelling the related form of the word.

Shrink the following words so that just the base word remains:
   a) **responsible**
   b) **original**
   c) i**ndependent**
   d) **prehistoric**

2. In Unit 33 we looked at the spelling problems created by vowels in unstressed syllables (schwa vowels). Many longer words contain vowels that are difficult to hear: opp**o**sition; def**i**nition.

A tactic that often works with such words is to return to the base form. Often the vowel is easy to hear in another form of the word: opp**o**sition—opp**o**se. Say both these words aloud.

Notice how the vowel in bold is hard to hear in the longer form but clear in the base word.

Write each word below. Beside each write the base word. Say both forms and listen for clues in the base to help you spell the longer form.
   a) **confident**
   b) **invitation**
   c) **competition**
   d) **composition**

Spelling Secret #34
Words that are related in **meaning** are usually related in **spelling**, even if they do not sound the same: sign—**sign**al; **sign**ature.

Putting the Secret to Work

1. Words with silent letters create spelling challenges. Sometimes it is possible to remember these letters by thinking of a related form of the word where the letter is not silent: si**g**n; si**g**nal; si**g**nature. Notice how the silent *g* in si**g**n can be heard in si**g**nal and si**g**nature.

For each word below write a related form in which the silent letter can be heard.

   a) mus**c**le
   b) resi**g**n
   c) bom**b**
   d) condem**n**

2. The words in the box all share the same base word **photo**.

> **photograph**   **photography**
> **photographic**   **photographer**

Complete each sentence with one of the words.

   a) The _____ took a picture of the famous actress.
   b) I would like to study _____ at college.
   c) People who remember every detail of an event are said to have a _____ memory.
   d) I remember when that _____ was taken.

3. The word **magician** means "someone who deals with **magic**." The same **ian** pattern is found in other words.

Complete the puzzle below with words ending in **ian**.

   Someone who deals with:
   a) music is a _____.
   b) politics is a _____.
   c) mathematics is a _____.
   d) physics (body) is a _____.
   e) cosmetics is a _____.

Slightly different patterns are shown below:

   Someone who deals with:
   f) electricity is an _____.
   g) beauty is a _____.
   h) diet is a _____.
   i) technology is a _____.

Home Connections

Collect a number of longer words from newspapers, magazines, and other reading materials. Ask your child to identify the base word in each. Brainstorm for other words that could be built on these base words.

Dictate the Unit and Challenge Words. Say each word clearly, read the sentence, and repeat the word.

Common Prefixes

Unit Words

interception	The other team made an **interception**.
interfere	Please don't **interfere** with my work.
intermediate	I'm learning **intermediate** level French.
international	The Olympics are an **international** event.
submarine	The **submarine** disappeared beneath the surface.
substitute	We had a **substitute** teacher today.
subtraction	These math problems involve **subtraction**.
suburban	The **suburban** town was near Toronto.
transcript	We read the **transcript** of the interview.
transition	The **transition** to high school can be scary.
translation	The **translation** was from English to French.
transportation	We used bus **transportation** for the trip.
uncertain	I am **uncertain** how to answer that question.
unemployment	The recession has led to high **unemployment**.
unfortunately	We are, **unfortunately**, unable to come today.

Challenge Words

intermission	We bought popcorn at the **intermission**.
subscription	Do you have a **subscription** to that magazine?
transparent	Window glass is **transparent**.
unconscious	The boxer was knocked **unconscious**.
unnatural	The new skates felt **unnatural** to me.

Rewrite any misspelled words. Pay close attention to any letters that gave you difficulty.

What's the Secret?

The prefixes **un** and **dis** usually make a word mean the opposite.

1. Make the following words mean the opposite by adding either **un** or **dis**.

a) **natural**	e) **appear**
b) **respectful**	f) **continued**
c) **fortunately**	g) **predictable**
d) **conscious**	h) **agreeable**

2. More than one prefix can be used with some base words. For example, the word **port** comes from Latin, meaning "to carry." Add the prefixes and suffixes below to the base word **port** to form as many words as possible. Notice how each prefix changes the meaning of the word:

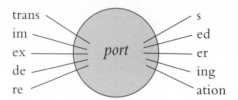

trans
im
ex
de
re

port

s
ed
er
ing
ation

Spelling Secret #35

The meaning and spelling of a word can be more easily understood when they are linked to the meaning of its prefix:

un usually means "not" and therefore changes the meaning of the base word to its opposite, as in **un**happy.

sub means "under" or "below," as in **sub**way

inter usually means "between," as in **inter**national (between nations)

trans usually means "across," as in **trans**port (carry across)

Putting the Secret to Work

1. A "transcript" is a written record. The base word is **scribe**, which comes from the Latin verb *scribere*, meaning "to write."

Before the invention of the printing press, a **scribe** was a person who copied manu**scripts** by hand. Combine any of the prefixes in the box with **scription** to complete the sentences below:

sub	pre	de	in

a) Do you have a _____ of the suspect?

b) What is the _____ on the trophy?

c) How many magazine _____ have you sold?

d) Did the doctor give you a _____ for your cold?

2. The prefix **inter** often means "between or among." Combine **inter** with each adjective on the outer circle. Then use each word correctly in one of the sentences below.

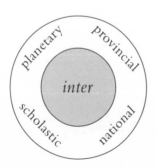

planetary provincial
inter
scholastic national

a) A track meet with competitors from Canada, Britain, and the United States is an _____ meet.

b) A space probe travelling from the planet Earth to the planet Mars is on an _____ space mission.

c) A meeting among premiers of British Columbia, Quebec, and Prince Edward Island is an _____ meeting.

d) A basketball game between Nelson High School and Blakelock High School is an _____ game.

3. Condense the following words to match the word clues. Use only letters found in the original word, but you may put them in any order.

For example: **compose**: something a writer might **compose** (4 letters)

answer: **poem**

a) **translation**: an ancient language that needs **translation** (5 letters)

b) **unemployment**: something you have less of when **unemployed** (5 letters)

c) **explore**: what a prospector might find (3 letters)

d) **intermission**: what performers do during **intermission** (4 letters)

Home Connections

The family can enjoy playing word games involving prefixes and suffixes. Focus on a specific prefix, such as **uni** or **trans**, and award a point for every word found with that prefix.

It is also a good opportunity to become more familiar with using the dictionary. Once the family has exhausted its own resources, go to the dictionary and add other words beginning with the same prefix. Be sure that the meaning of each word is also understood.

UNIT 36

Common Suffixes

Dictate the Unit and Challenge Words. Say each word clearly, read the sentence, and repeat the word.

Unit Words

arrangement	Do you like this flower **arrangement**?
awareness	Safety **awareness** is very important.
carelessness	You could be injured through **carelessness**.
competition	We entered the short story **competition**.
conclusion	What is the **conclusion** to your experiment?
decision	Have you come to a **decision** yet?
definition	What is the **definition** of this term?
division	We are learning how to do long **division**.
forgiveness	I can only ask for your **forgiveness**.
imagination	Use your **imagination** for this drawing.
immigration	The newcomer filled out **immigration** papers.
introduction	I wrote an **introduction** for my speech.

nervousness   My shaking hands showed my **nervousness**.

opposition   There was much **opposition** to the new law.

requirement   A valid licence is a **requirement** for driving.

Challenge Words

admission   What is the **admission** cost for the movie?

disappointment   Their **disappointment** at losing was obvious.

exhibition   There was a skating **exhibition** yesterday.

harassment   Any form of **harassment** is unacceptable.

repetition   **Repetition** can help learning.

Remember the silent *h* in **exhibition**.

Rewrite any misspelled words. Pay close attention to any letters that gave you difficulty.

What's the Secret?

1. Add the suffix shown to each of the base words below.

     a) **require + ment**

     b) **careless + ness**

     c) **harass + ment**

     d) **nervous + ness**

Notice that in each case the suffix was added with no change to the base word.

2. Add the given suffix to these words. This time pay attention to the changes made to the base word.

     a) **conclude + sion**

     b) **admit + sion**

     c) **imagine + ation**

     d) **divide + sion**

3. In Units 34 and 35 we looked at vowels in unstressed syllables (schwa vowels) and noticed they are difficult to hear clearly.

Write each of the Unit and Challenge Words below. Highlight the **boldface** schwa vowel in some way—different colour ink, or circle it. Beside each write the base word. Highlight the same vowel in the base word. Notice that the vowel is easy to hear in the base form.

     a) comp**e**tition

     b) def**i**nition

     c) opp**o**sition

     d) rep**e**tition

Spelling Secret #36

The meaning and spelling of a longer word can be more easily understood when they are linked to the base word:

     opposition—oppose; introduction—introduce.

Putting the Secret to Work

1. Add the suffix **ness** to the word in bold in the first sentence of each pair below. Then use this word to complete the second sentence.

For example: Our new German shepherd seems very **happy**. He shows his **happiness** by wagging his tail and barking.

a) Are you **aware** of the courses being offered at night school? This pamphlet should increase your _____.

b) You shouldn't be so **careless**. Your _____ could cause an accident.

c) Will you **forgive** me for being late again? I know I don't deserve your _____.

d) I can tell you are **nervous**. Your tapping fingers and fidgety feet show your _____.

e) My friend Sarah is a pleasant person but she's very **lazy**. Her _____ cost her a good summer job.

Colour these letters; draw them larger; use a highlighter pen, etc.

2. The Unit and Challenge Words in the box all have double consonants. Write each word and highlight the double consonants so they will stand out in your memory.

ha**ra**ssment	disa**pp**ointment
a**rr**angement	i**mm**igration
o**pp**osition	admi**ss**ion

3. How many words can you make by adding suffixes to each base word in the circle? At least two suffixes can be added to each base.

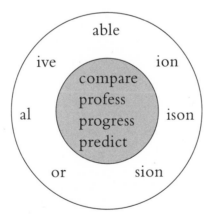

Home Connections

Make it a family game to look for the longest real words in the language. These words will almost certainly be built on prefixes and suffixes. A word such as "counterrevolution" may seem very difficult to read and to spell, but when it is broken down into **counter + revolution**, it is manageable. When your child understands the meaning of common prefixes, the meaning of many longer words will also become apparent.

Dictate the Unit and Challenge Words. Say each word clearly, read the sentence, and repeat the word.

Words Borrowed from Other Languages

Unit Words

banana	In the morning I eat a fresh **banana**.
cashier	The store manager hired a new **cashier**.
coffee	Would you care for a cup of **coffee**?
crystal	The cookies were served on a **crystal** platter.
knuckle	The old woman's **knuckle** was badly swollen.
ozone	There is a hole in the **ozone** layer.
pretzel	I ate a warm **pretzel** at the movies.
raccoon	A **raccoon** is living in our backyard.
reindeer	The caribou is a North American **reindeer**.
schedule	Do you have a busy **schedule** today?
snorkel	I love to use a **snorkel** in shallow water.
syrup	Maple **syrup** is one of the treats of spring.
tornado	A strong **tornado** damaged the city.
typhoon	The island was devastated by the **typhoon**.
yacht	They sailed to the Caribbean in their **yacht**.

Challenge Words

barbecue	I like to **barbecue** steak in the summer.
caterpillar	The **caterpillar** crawled up the leaf.
limousine	They went to the dance in a **limousine**.
moccasin	The **moccasin** was made from soft leather.
sarcasm	"Yeah, right," she said with **sarcasm**.

sarcasm—from Greek "sarkazein"—"to tear flesh"!

Rewrite any misspelled words. Pay close attention to any letters that gave you difficulty.

What's the Secret?

1. The Unit and Challenge Words originate from many languages. Try to match the words with their languages of origin.

You may find clues in a dictionary. Otherwise, the answers are in Appendix III!

a) French	1._____	2._____	3._____
b) Greek	1._____	2._____	3._____
c) Spanish	1._____	2._____	
d) Dutch	1._____	2._____	
e) Arabic	1._____	2._____	
f) German	1._____	2._____	
g) American Indian	1._____	2._____	
h) Old Norse	1._____		
i) West African	1._____		
j) Chinese	1._____		
k) Latin	1._____		

Putting the Secret to Work

Because these words come from many languages they often use unfamiliar combinations of letters. It is important to develop tactics beyond just sounding these words out. The activities below show a number of approaches to remembering the spelling of the Unit and Challenge Words.

1. Shape: Match the words in the box with the configurations (shapes) below.

crystal	knuckle	syrup
typhoon	yacht	pretzel

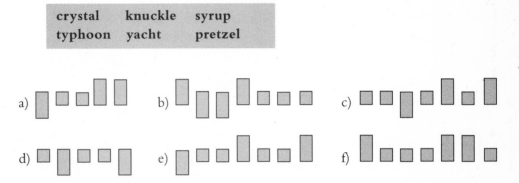

a)   b)   c)

d)   e)   f)

caterpillar—comes from Old French *chatte peleuse* meaning "hairy cat"

2. Double consonants: Complete the puzzle below with Unit and Challenge Words containing double consonants.

Highlight the double consonants.

a)   __ __ **ff** __ __

b)   __ __ **cc** __ __ __

c)   __ __ **cc** __ __ __ __

d)   __ __ __ __ __ __ __ **ll** __ __

3. Mnemonics (memory tricks): Mnemonic tricks are designed to remind you of specific letters in a word. For example, you could remember the beginning of **schedule** by saying, "At **sch**ool I have a **sch**edule."

Create some mnemonic tricks to help you with the difficult parts of some Unit or Challenge Words. For example, how will you remember that **moccasin** has two c's?

barbecue—Spanish via Haitian *barbacoa*—"a framework for roasting"

4. Vowel combinations: Complete the words below with the correct vowels:

a) **lim __ __ sine**

b) **cash __ __ r**

c) **r __ __ ndeer**

d) **barbec __ __**

5. Some English words were borrowed directly from other languages. For example, **igloo** comes from an Inuit word *iglu*, meaning "a dwelling." The technical term for word origins is "etymology." In a dictionary entry this feature is often shortened to **Etym**.

Use a dictionary to find the origin of these words. Name the language from which the word was borrowed and the meaning of the word in that language.

    a) **toboggan**
    b) **malaria**
    c) **chipmunk**

Home Connections

Many scientific names are based on Greek roots. Your family can have fun creating and drawing imaginary creatures based on these roots.

root	meaning
octa	eight
mono	one
tri	three
diplo	double
chromo	colour
icthyo	fish
dactylo	finger
rhino	nose
derm	skin
odont	tooth
pod	foot

6 Special Challenges

Special Challenges

Introduction

The mark of a first-rate speller is the ability to go beyond what makes sense in the spelling system of English and to master what does not make sense. Although there are many aspects of English spelling that are logical, it is one of the most difficult languages to spell. That is because there is often a difference between how a word is said in English and how it is spelled.

Section 6, the final set of units in this book, focuses on special spelling challenges. Words are grouped on the basis of silent letters, double consonants, unusual vowel combinations, pairs of words easily confused, and those that are difficult to pronounce.

To deal with the spelling of such challenging words, it is necessary to use a wide variety of spelling tactics. These tactics will include visual strategies, for "seeing" the word clearly; auditory approaches, for "hearing" the word; and memory tactics, for recalling the word through memory tricks. Although these tactics will be used to learn the spelling of specific words, they can be applied to any words you face that do not follow simple spelling rules or patterns.

The final "secret" to share, therefore, is that becoming a top-notch speller is not easy. It takes time to become aware of the many levels of the English spelling system and the rules and patterns that apply to each. It takes patience to develop tactics for the many challenges created by words that don't follow these patterns. Although some people seem to find spelling easier than others, very few people are born good spellers. No matter what your natural talent in this area, careful study and persistence will result in better spelling performance. We hope this book will continue to move you further along your own path to spelling success.

UNIT 38

Words with Silent Letters

Dictate the Unit and Challenge Words. Say each word clearly, read the sentence, and repeat the word.

Unit Words

answer	She knew the **answer** to the math question.
autumn	In **autumn** the colours are beautiful.
awkward	I felt **awkward** when I couldn't remember him.
debt	Our club has a large **debt** to pay.
doubt	I **doubt** that you are telling the truth.
exhaust	The **exhaust** fumes had a foul smell.
jealous	He was **jealous** of his friend's success.
knock	There was a loud **knock** at the door.

lawyer	The **lawyer** argued the case effectively.
pumpkin	One of my favourite desserts is **pumpkin** pie.
scissors	Be careful how you carry the **scissors**.
climbed	We were tired after we **climbed** the hill.
walking	A good form of exercise is **walking**.
vacuum	I have to **vacuum** my room before I can go out.
vehicle	The storm led to a ten-**vehicle** accident.

Challenge Words

daughter	His **daughter** was coming home for a visit.
foreign	Do you speak a **foreign** language?
knowledge	We gained a lot of **knowledge** on the field trip.
mortgage	You can get a **mortgage** at the bank.
receipt	I kept my **receipt** when I bought the coat.

Remember that a **lawyer** deals with the **law**.

Rewrite any misspelled words. Pay close attention to any letters that gave you difficulty.

What's the Secret?

1. Sometimes it helps to remember a silent letter by pretending it is sounded. For example, when you want to spell **leopard**, remember the silent *o* by saying to yourself, "lee-o-pard." Say these Unit and Challenge Words aloud so that the silent letter can be heard:

mortgage   s**c**issors   ans**w**er

2. Silent letters in a base word can often be heard in a related form of the word. Notice how the silent *c* in the word mus**c**le is sounded in the related form mus**c**ular.

For example: bom**b**—bom**b**ard

The following base words all end in **mn**, with the **n** silent. Write a related form of each word so that the **n** can be heard. Consult a dictionary if you need help.

a) colum**n** ⟶ colum**n**_____
b) autum**n** ⟶ autum**n**_____
c) condem**n** ⟶ condem**n**_____

3. Some silent letters can best be remembered by recalling the overall shape of the word. If you know, for example, that there is a "high" letter in the word **exhaust**, it is easier to remember the silent **h**.
Match the shapes below with the words in the box.

| debt | daughter | vehicle |
| pumpkin | doubt | mortgage |

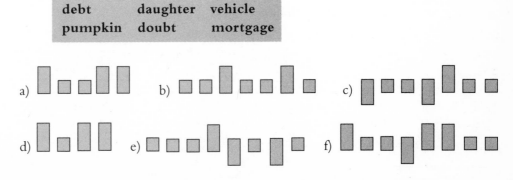

a)   b)   c)

d)   e)   f)

Putting the Secret to Work

1. The words **knock** and **knowledge** contain a silent *k* at the beginning. The
kn pattern is fairly common in English.

Complete the following puzzle with words beginning with **kn**. Use the
numbered clues to answer the "Knock Knock" joke at the end.

a) Part of your finger   kn _ _ _ _ _
                            3 4   1 2

b) Rhymes with **grown**   kn _ _ _
                              5

c) A sharp weapon   kn _ _ _
                       6 7

d) Press and squeeze dough   kn _ _ _
                                8 9

e) Medieval soldier   kn _ _ _ _
                         10

f) Handle of a door   kn _ _
                         11

g) Full of knots   kn _ _ _ _
                      12

Knock, knock! Who's there? Lettuce. Lettuce who?

__ __ __ __ __ __ __   __ __   __ __ __
 1 2 10 10 3 4 2   6 5   8 5 9
__ __ __ __ __   __ __ __ __   __ __ __ !
12 11 3   1 1   7 6 5 9   11 3 10

2. Complete the following Unit and Challenge Words with the correct vowel
combinations.

a) **rec __ __ pt**
b) **for __ __ gn**
c) **j __ __ lous**
d) **vac __ __ m**

Home Connections

It is important for you and your children to discuss the tactics you use to spell
difficult words. Poor spellers tend to use only a limited number of tactics—they
sound the word out, look at it, perhaps write it out.

The activities above help you to notice more specific details about the words
and give you tactics that can be applied to other words.

Words with Double Consonants

Dictate the Unit and Challenge Words. Say each word clearly, read the sentence, and repeat the word.

Unit Words

blizzard	There was a **blizzard** at the ski resort.
different	Can you think of a **different** answer?
hurricane	The **hurricane** tore up trees and houses.
irrigation	Farmers need a good **irrigation** system.
marriage	They announced their **marriage** plans.
occasion	The wedding will be a wonderful **occasion**.
official	This is an **official** major league bat.
possession	Do you have the diamond in your **possession**?
rabbit	The **rabbit** blended in with the snow.
stubborn	The horse was unruly and **stubborn**.
sufficient	Would five dollars be **sufficient**?
suggestion	What a wonderful **suggestion**!
terrific	I'm afraid I have a **terrific** headache.
tomorrow	I may not be in school **tomorrow**.
village	The **village** was crowded with skiers.

Challenge Words

accidentally	Did you break that cup **accidentally**?
appointment	Don't forget your dental **appointment**.
dilemma	That problem posed quite a **dilemma**.
exaggerate	Sometimes I tend to **exaggerate** things.
interrupt	Please don't **interrupt** when I'm speaking.

Rewrite any misspelled words. Pay close attention to any letters that gave you difficulty.

What's the Secret?

1. Look at each Unit and Challenge Word. What is common to each of these words? Now examine your Pretest. Were any of your errors due to double consonants? If so, rewrite these words correctly and circle the double consonants.

Spelling Secret #39

It is important to develop tactics such as memory tricks to remember the double consonants in words such as **occasion** and **interrupt**.

Putting the Secret to Work

1. If the double consonants in a word are letters that are above or below the line (for example: **g**, **t**, **p**, **l**), studying the shape of the whole word is one tactic for remembering the spelling.

Match the shapes below with the Unit and Challenge Words shown.

official	exaggerate	village	stubborn
suggestion	rabbit	sufficient	appointment

a)   b)

c)   d)

e)   f)

g)   h)

2. Configuration is not an effective tactic for remembering double consonants such as **r**, **c**, or **s**. These consonants can often be remembered by leaving blanks in the word and completing them in a special way: e.g., using a different colour of ink or highlighter pen, circling them, using capital letters or a different script.

Use one of these tactics to complete the Unit and Challenge Words below. Concentrate on the double consonants as you write them.

a) **bli __ __ ard**   b) **hu __ __ icane**

c) **inte __ __ upt**   d) **a __ __ identally**

e) **te __ __ ific**   f) **i __ __ igation**

g) **o __ __ asion**   h) **po __ __ e __ __ ion**

i) **ma __ __ iage**   j) **tomo __ __ ow**

k) **dile __ __ a**

3. A word can sometimes be drawn in a way that reminds us of the tricky letters.

Try drawing some of the Unit and Challenge Words so that the double consonants are obvious. Start with **giraffe**!

4. Write the base word for each of the Unit and Challenge Words below:

a) **accidentally**   b) **appointment**

c) **suggestion**   d) **irrigation**

e) **possession**   f) **sufficient**

Notice how the double **l**'s in **accidentally** make sense when you begin with the base word and add suffixes. For example:

accident + al = accidental

accidental + ly = accidentally

5. Memory tricks (also called mnemonic devices) sometimes help us to remember double consonants. For example, you can remember the double set of **s**'s in po**ss**e**ss**ion by saying, "Her most valuable po**ss**e**ss**ion is a **s**pecial **s**et of **s**terling **s**ilver."

A common mistake in spelling **occasion** is doubling the **s** instead of the **c**; likewise, in **tomorrow**, the **m** is often doubled instead of the **r**.

Can you think of a mnemonic trick to remember which letter is doubled in each case?

Home Connections

Use letters from commercial games such as Scrabble® or Boggle® to assemble words with double consonants. Give bonus credit for words with more than one set of double consonants, as in **possession**.

U N I T 4 0

Dictate the Unit and Challenge Words. Say each word clearly, read the sentences, and repeat the word.

Pronunciation Challenges

Unit Words

adjective	An **adjective** is a describing word.
arctic	An **arctic** air mass made it bitterly cold.
depth	The **depth** of the river was two metres.
drawer	Your socks are in the top **drawer**.
escape	The hamster tried to **escape** from his cage.
extinct	The dodo bird is an **extinct** species.
February	The second month of the year is **February**.
length	She swam the **length** of the pool.
lightning	The tree was struck by **lightning**.
nuclear	There has been a reduction in **nuclear** weapons.
raspberry	My favourite berry is a **raspberry**.
realize	Do you **realize** how much this is worth?
recognize	I don't believe you **recognize** me.
valuable	That was a **valuable** lesson in safety.
Wednesday	Are you going to the movies on **Wednesday**?

Challenge Words

exception	There is one **exception** to the rule.
laboratory	The scientist worked in the **laboratory**.
mischievous	My little brother is quite **mischievous**.
particularly	This package is **particularly** heavy.
pronunciation	The **pronunciation** of that word is difficult.

Rewrite any misspelled words. Pay close attention to any letters that gave you difficulty.

What's the Secret?

1. Some of the Unit and Challenge Words are often misspelled because we fail to pronounce them clearly in everyday speech.

Say the following words clearly. Look at each word as you say it. Notice the letters that are sometimes slurred or not pronounced.

arctic	February	adjective
depth	recognize	extinct

Spelling Secret #40

Some words are difficult to spell because they are often mispronounced in everyday speech. Others, such as **Wednesday**, are not spelled as they are said. Special tactics, related to pronunciation, are needed for remembering the spelling of these words.

Putting the Secret to Work

*Notice that when **pronounce** becomes **pronunciation** the o is dropped from the middle.*

1. The following words may be easier to remember if each syllable is noticed. Unscramble the syllables to find Unit and Challenge Words.

a) ci•nun•a•pro•tion
b) tic•lar•ly•par•u
c) u•val•ble•a
d) ra•to•lab•ry•o

2. Some words have letters that can best be remembered by purposely exaggerating or mispronouncing the sounds. For example: s**c**issors—say "**skissors**" to remember the silent **c.**

Say the following Unit and Challenge Words so that the underlined letters can be heard.

a) Wed**nes**day
b) lab**o**ratory
c) ras**p**berry
d) val**u**able
e) dra**w**er

3. Add the suffixes indicated to build the base word **except** to **exceptionally**.

a) **except + ion** =
b) **exception + al** =
c) **exceptional + ly** =

4. Build as many words as possible on the base word **real**.

5. Some words are often spoken carelessly so that sounds are not in the proper sequence. Read the Unit Words below so that each sound is heard in the correct order.

a) **nuclear**
b) **escape**
c) **mischievous**
d) **extinct**

6. Match the shapes below with the Unit Words shown.

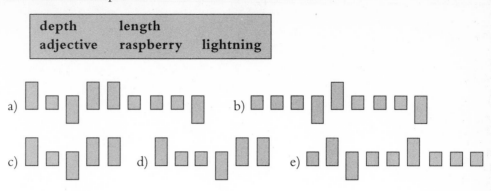

depth	length	
adjective	raspberry	lightning

Home Connections

Utilize the tactics in this unit whenever you and your child come upon a word that is not clearly pronounced. Discuss tricks for remembering the difficult parts of the word, especially silent letters or the middle portion of a word, which is often not clearly heard in normal speech.

UNIT 41

Words Often Confused

Dictate the Unit and Challenge Words. Say each word clearly, read the sentences, and repeat the word.

Unit Words

angel	We made **angel** figures in the snow.
angle	The tree was bent at an odd **angle**.
breath	After running I had to catch my **breath**.
breathe	He choked on the meat and couldn't **breathe**.
close	Would you please **close** the window?
clothes	We'll need to dress in warm **clothes**.
dairy	I went to the **dairy** for some milk.
diary	The explorer kept a detailed **diary**.
dessert	What is your favourite **dessert**?
desert	Las Vegas is in the middle of a **desert**.
loose	The sweatshirt was very **loose**.
lose	Did you **lose** your keys again?
rhyme	The lines of a poem don't have to **rhyme**.
rhythm	The toddler danced to the **rhythm** of the music.

Challenge Words

accept	Will you **accept** this token of thanks?
except	Everyone **except** my dad likes this program.
personal	Don't share this note—it's **personal**.
personnel	I was hired by the manager of **personnel**.
quiet	The teacher asked us to be **quiet**.
quite	That was **quite** a show of strength!

Rewrite any misspelled words. Pay close attention to any letters that gave you difficulty.

What's the Secret?

1. Certain pairs of words are often confused in English. It is important to distinguish between them for both reading and spelling. Complete each sentence with the correct words in the brackets.

a) The (**angel/angle**) was tied to the top of the tree on an (**angel/angle**).

b) He found himself out of (**breath/breathe**) during the race; by the time he crossed the finish line he could barely (**breath/breathe**).

c) Because my sister and I are so (**clothes/close**) in size, we can share the same (**clothes/close**).

d) I recorded twenty trips to the (**diary/dairy**) in my summer (**diary/dairy**).

e) If I were lost in the (**desert/dessert**) my favourite (**desert/dessert**) would be a giant ice cream cone.

f) The (**loose/lose**) puck deflected into our net and caused us to (**loose/lose**) the game.

g) Even though the lines do not (**rhythm/rhyme**), my poem still has (**rhythm/rhyme**).

h) The teacher would not (**accept/except**) any late papers (**accept/except**) those that came with a slip from the office.

i) The (**personnel/personal**) officer did not ask any (**personnel/personal**) questions during the interview.

j) There is (**quiet/quite**) a difference between the (**quiet/quite**) morning streets and the afternoon traffic jams.

Spelling Secret #41

A variety of memory tactics may be needed to distinguish between words that are easily confused in English.

Putting the Secret to Work

1. Sometimes the best way to tell these word pairs apart is to create nonsense sentences with memory clues in them.

For example: I tried a qu**iet** d**iet** of cheese and bread.

That was qu**ite** a k**ite** !

Try to design some memory tricks for the other word pairs in the Unit and Challenge lists. Keep a list and add to it as you think of mnemonics for other words.

2. Many of the confusing word pairs in the Unit and Challenge Words have only one or two letters that are different. In some cases, the same letters are used but in a different order.

Complete the puzzle with the correct words.

a) **d __ __ ry**   a journal; record of events
b) **d __ __ ry**   a business that sells milk
c) **ang __ __**   in certain religions, a messenger of God
d) **ang __ __**   a geometric term
e) **qui __ __**   opposite of noisy
f) **qui __ __**   very much; entirely
g) **__ __ cept**   leaving out; other than
h) **__ __ cept**   consent to take; say yes to

3. Both **accept** and **except** are base words to which suffixes can be added. Complete the following passage with words from the box.

exception	acceptance
exceptional	acceptable

Have you received a letter of _____ from the college? Your marks are _____, with the _____ perhaps of physics. I wouldn't worry, though, because your letters of reference are absolutely_____.

Home Connections

It may be helpful to keep a special page in your spelling record or notebook for confusing word pairs. Use each word in a sentence for easy reference.

UNIT 42

Unusual Vowel Combinations

Dictate the Unit and Challenge Words. Say each word clearly, read the sentence, and repeat the word.

Unit Words

biscuit	The dog chewed on his **biscuit**.
canoe	The man was paddling his **canoe** on the lake.
circuit	The equipment caused a short **circuit**.
cocoa	Would you like a cup of hot **cocoa**?
diamond	She was given a **diamond** ring by her husband.
feud	There was a bitter **feud** in the neighbourhood.
leisure	What do you do in your **leisure** time?
pageant	We staged a **pageant** for our medieval fair.
penguin	The **penguin** shuffled across the ice.
rescue	Great courage was shown in the **rescue**.
soldier	The **soldier** was injured in the battle.
surgeon	He was operated on by the **surgeon** on duty.

tongue	I bit my **tongue**!
tortoise	The **tortoise** raced against the hare.
Tuesday	The movie is cheaper on **Tuesday**.

Challenge Words

leopard	The **leopard** belongs to the cat family.
lieutenant	The **lieutenant** ordered the soldiers to move.
miniature	He held a **miniature** sculpture in his hand.
parliament	The new **parliament** met soon after the election.
restaurant	She went to the **restaurant** with her friends.

Rewrite any misspelled words. Pay close attention to any letters that gave you difficulty.

What's the Secret?

1. Look carefully at each of the Unit and Challenge Words. Notice the two or more vowels side by side in each word. These particular vowel combinations are not found frequently in English spelling. In many cases, the words have been borrowed from other languages, as in "**lieu**tenant," which comes from French. There are no simple ways of remembering these unusual vowel combinations. Configuration or shape will not help since these vowels are neither above nor below the line. Sounding the word out is also of limited value.

> ### Spelling Secret #42
> Some words contain unusual vowel combinations. A variety of visual tactics need to be used to remember the spelling of these words. Many must be learned word by word.

Putting the Secret to Work

The following tactics may help you to concentrate on the key letters in these words. Many of them stress a visual approach.

1. Complete the following words by adding the correct vowels. Highlight these letters in some way as an aid to memory.

pag __ __ nt	sold __ __ r
rest __ __ rant	f __ __ d
tort __ __ se	l __ __ __ tenant
coc __ __	can __ __

2. The word **leisure** is one of the exceptions to the "i before e except after c" rule.

Look carefully at other exceptions to this pattern:

for**ei**gn	forf**ei**t
h**ei**ght	w**ei**rd
n**ei**ther	s**ei**ze
consc**ie**nce	

3. The words needed to complete the puzzles below share common vowel patterns.

Solve each puzzle with Unit and Challenge Words.

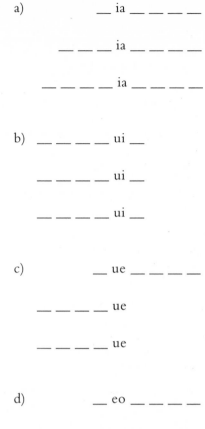

a) __ ia __ __ __ __

   __ __ __ ia __ __ __ __

   __ __ __ __ ia __ __ __ __

b) __ __ __ __ ui __

   __ __ __ __ ui __

   __ __ __ __ ui __

c) __ ue __ __ __ __

   __ __ __ __ ue

   __ __ __ __ ue

d) __ eo __ __ __ __

   __ __ __ __ eo __

4. Sometimes knowing the origin of a word aids in its spelling.
For example, the word **leopard** comes from the ancient Greek word
"*leopardos,*" which meant a "lion panther": **leon** ("lion") + **pardos** ("panther")
That is why there's a silent *e* in **leopard**!

Home Connections

Use all of these tactics regularly as you seek to become a world-class speller.
Also remember the spelling techniques used in the previous units. Find out
which tactics work best for you so that you are never stumped by a new word.
You will know how to examine the word carefully and use the best tactics for
remembering any difficult parts.

Good luck!

Appendices

Appendix I

The 200 Words Most Frequently Misspelled
(based on a random sample of 3,540 compositions written by adults as well as children in Canada)

about
accident
actually
afraid
again
all
almost
always
and
animals
another
are
around
away
awhile
back
bear
beautiful
because
been
before
began
behind
believe
better
bird
birthday
brought
built
buys
bye
came
can't
catch
caught
certainly

chases
children
climbed
come
coming
could
couldn't
cousins
decided
didn't
different
doctor
does
doesn't
dollars
don't
engine
equipment
especially
ever
every
everybody
everyday
everything
exciting
family
fell
few
field
finally
finished
fired
first
flowers
for
found
funny
friend
girls
going
government
happened
happily
having
heard
here
him
his

hole
home
horses
hospital
house
I'm
into
its
it's
just
knew
know
let's
like
lived
looked
met
middle
might
minute
months
mountains
myself
names
necessary
neighbour
next
no
nothing
now
o'clock
off
once
one
opportunity
others
our
out
outside
parents
parliament
people
picked
pictures
piece
place
pollution
practicing

pretty
probably
quiet
quite
really
receive
responsible
right
said
saw
scared
school
screamed
second
shoot
shot
situation
slept
so
society
some
something
sometimes
spotted
started
stepped
stopped
strange
summer
surely
surprise
swimming
take
than
that's
the
their
them
then
there
there's
they
they're
things
thought
threw
throw
to
too

tried
turned
two
until
upon
very
wanted
wasn't
went
we're
were
weren't
what's
when
where
without
wouldn't
writing
you're

The 200 Words Most Frequently written
(in descending order of frequency)

the
and
I
a
to
was
in
it
he
my
we
of
is
you
they
on
that
went
when
for
so
one
then
she
said
but
there
had
me
have
with
are
all
got
go
like
day
were
out
up

his
at
him
her
be
get
would
home
not
some
came
saw
if
as
because
going
what
time
will
very
do
down
them
about
back
our
can
two
after
house
dog
little
from
could
mother
people
into
just
over
see
now
or
school
their
play
an
by
come

big
did
no
man
am
good
too
once
ran
name
know
took
how
who
started
put
old
night
has
your
off
us
around
next
other
well
away
fun
three
cat
where
Mom
told
boy
Dad
again
found
more
nice
friends
way
think
asked
friend
father
looked
summer
first

made
never
here
didn't
want
right
horse
don't
car
heard
called
why
door
something
take
water
only
long
morning
five
make
things
I'm
girl
much
years
bed
lot
look
four
lived
many
fish
new
thought
always
bear
tree
wanted
place
yes
really
eat
last
left
oh
it's
thing

another
through
find
say
black
run
gave
even
should
best

Appendix II

d — t
bed—bet
bid—bit
rod—rot
cud—cut

Short Vowel
Pairs
a — e
sat—set
mat—met
pan—pen
a — i
fat—fit
hat—hit
sat—sit
a — o
jab—job
pat—pot
rat—rot
a — u
bat—but
cat—cut
ran—run
e — i
bet—bit
set—sit
wet—wit
e — o
beg—bog
get—got
pet—pot
e — u
bet—but
hem—hum
leg—lug
i — o
din—Don
rib—rob
rid—rod
i — u
bin—bun
fin—fun
pin—pun
o — u
cub—cob
rub—rob
sub—sob

UNIT 2:
Word Families
with **g, b,**
and **t**

Words
ending in **t**
at
bat
cat
pat
sat
et
bet
get
jet
wet
it
bit
fit
hit
pit
ot
dot
got
hot
pot
ut
but
cut
hut
nut

Words ending
in **b**
ab
cab
jab
lab
grab
ib
bib
fib
rib
crib
ob
cob
job
rob

sob
ub
cub
hub
rub
tub

Words ending
in **g**
ag
bag
rag
tag
wag
eg
beg
keg
leg
peg
ig
big
dig
pig
wig
og
bog
dog
fog
log
ug
bug
hug
mug
rug

UNIT 3:
Word Families
with **d** and **m**

Words ending
in **d**
ad
bad
had
mad
sad
ed
bed
fed

led
red
id
did
hid
kid
rid
od
cod
nod
rod
sod
ud
bud
mud
stud
thud

Words ending
in **m**
am
ham
jam
ram
yam
em
gem
hem
stem
them
im
dim
him
brim
swim
um
gum
hum
sum
drum

UNIT 4:
Word Families
with **n, p** and **x**

Words ending
in **n**
an
can

man
pan
ran
en
hen
men
ten
then
in
bin
pin
tin
win
un
fun
gun
run
sun

Words ending
in **p**
ap
cap
map
rap
tap
ip
dip
lip
rip
zip
op
cop
hop
mop
top
up
cup
pup
syrup

Words ending
in **x**
ax
fax
tax
wax

ix
fix
mix
six
ox
box
fox
lox

UNIT 5:
Short Vowels and Consonant Combinations— **ck, ch tch, st, sh**

Words ending in **ck**
ack
back
pack
black
track
eck
deck
neck
check
wreck
ick
pick
sick
quick
stick
ock
clock
lock
rock
sock
uck
buck
duck
luck
truck

Words ending in **ch**
much
such
which
rich

Words ending in **nch**
branch
bench
French

pinch
bunch
punch
lunch

Words ending in **tch**
atch
batch
catch
match
scratch
itch
ditch
pitch
witch
switch
otch
notch
blotch
Scotch
utch
Dutch
hutch
clutch
crutch

Words ending in **st**
ast
fast
last
past
vast
est
best
nest
rest
west
ist
fist
list
mist
wrist
ost
cost
lost
frost
ust
dust
just
must
rust

Words ending in **sh**
ash
cash
crash
dash
splash
ish
dish
fish
swish
wish
ush
brush
crush
gush
hush

UNIT 6:
Word Families with Double Consonants

Words ending in **ll**
all
ball
call
fall
tall
ell
bell
cell
fell
tell
ill
bill
fill
kill
will
ull
dull
gull
hull

Words ending in **ff**
iff
cliff
sniff
stiff
whiff
uff
cuff
fluff
puff
stuff

Words ending in **ss**
ass
class
grass
mass
pass
ess
guess
less
mess
press
iss
bliss
hiss
kiss
miss
oss
boss
loss
moss
toss
uss
cuss
fuss
muss
truss

Words ending in **mp**
amp
camp
champ
damp
stamp
omp
chomp
pomp
stomp
romp
ump
dump
jump
lump
pump

UNIT 7:
Short Vowels and Consonant Combinations— **nd, ng, nt, nk**

Words ending in **nd**
and
hand

land
sand
stand
end
bend
lend
mend
send

Words ending in **ng**
ang
bang
gang
rang
sang
ing
ring
sing
thing
wing
ong
gong
song
tong
wrong
ung
lung
rung
stung
sung

Words ending in **nk**
ank
bank
drank
tank
thank
ink
drink
rink
sink
think
unk
bunk
drunk
junk
trunk

Words ending in **nt**
ant
chant
grant
pant
plant

ent
bent
cent
sent
went
int
hint
mint
print
tint
unt
blunt
grunt
hunt
stunt

UNIT 8:
Long Vowels **a** and **o**
Words ending in **a**—consonant—**e**

ace
face
place
race
space
ade
grade
made
shade
trade
ake
bake
lake
take
wake
ame
game
name
same
tame
ate
date
hate
late
mate

Words ending in **o**—consonant—**e**
ode
code
rode
mode

strode
oke
Coke
choke
joke
spoke
ole
hole
pole
role
stole
ome
dome
home
chrome
gnome
one
bone
cone
phone
stone
ose
chose
nose
rose
those

UNIT 9:
Word Families
with Long **i**

Words ending
in **i**—conso-
nant—**e**
ice
mice
nice
price
rice
ide
hide
ride
side
wide
ife
life
knife
strife
wife
ike
bike
hike
like
strike
ile
file

pile
mile
smile
ime
dime
crime
lime
time
ine
fine
line
mine
nine
ipe
pipe
ripe
stripe
wipe
ite
bite
kite
white
write
ive
dive
five
hive
drive

UNIT 10:
Long **e** as in *bee*
— e, ee, ea, ey

Words with
long **e** spelled **e**
e
be
he
me
she
we

Words with
long **e** spelled
ee
ee
bee
free
see
tree
eed
bleed
feed
speed
weed
eek

cheek
creek
seek
week
eel
feel
heel
steel
wheel
een
been
green
queen
seen
eep
deep
creep
sleep
weep
eet
feet
greet
meet
sheet

Words with
long **e** spelled
ea
each
beach
peach
reach
teach
eak
beak
peak
speak
weak
eal
deal
meal
real
steal
eam
dream
team
scream
team
ean
bean
clean
jean
mean
eat
beat
cheat

neat
seat

Words with
long **e** spelled
ey
donkey
hockey
key
monkey
turkey

UNIT 11:
Long **a** — **ay,**
ai

Words with
long **a** spelled
ay
day
may
pay
say
way

Words with
long **a** spelled **ai**
ail
bail
fail
mail
pail
sail
ain
gain
main
pain
rain
vain
aid
aid
braid
laid
paid
raid

UNIT 12:
Long **i** — **ie, y,**
igh

Words with
long **i** spelled **ie**
die
lie
pie
tie

Words with
long **i** spelled **y**
y
by
cry
dry
fly
my

Words with
long **i** spelled
igh
ight
fight
bright
might
night
sight

UNIT 13:
Long **o** — **o,**
oa, ow

Words with
long **o** spelled **o**
go
ho
no
so

Words with
long **o** spelled
ow
blow
grow
low
show
throw

Words with
long **o** spelled
oa
oad
load
road
toad
oal
foal
goal
shoal
oat
boat
coat
float
throat

UNIT 14:
Long **u** — **o,**
oo, ew, ue

Words with
long **u** spelled **o**
do
to
two
who

Words with
long **u** spelled
ew
blew
dew
few
grew
new

Words with
long **u** spelled
ue
blue
clue
glue
true

Words with
long **u** spelled
oo
ool
cool
fool
pool
tool
school
oom
boom
broom
gloom
room
zoom
oon
goon
loon
moon
noon
soon
oop
droop
hoop
loop
scoop
troop

oot
hoot
loot
toot
scoot
shoot

R—CONTROLLED VOWELS

UNIT 15:
Short **a** + **r**,
Short **o** + **r**

Words with
short **ar**
ar
bar
car
far
jar
star
ark
bark
dark
mark
park
shark
arm
arm
charm
farm
harm
art
chart
dart
part
tart
start

Words with
short **or** spelled
or
orch
porch
scorch
torch
orn
born
corn
horn
thorn
ort
fort
port

sort
short
sport

Words ending
in short **or**
spelled **ore**
bore
core
more
score
store

Words with
short **or** spelled
ar
war
warble
ward
warm
warmth

UNIT 16:
Words ending
in **er**

Agents (people
who do things)
ending in **er**
baker
batter
catcher
carpenter
dancer
farmer
helper
lawyer
miner
painter
player
plumber
singer
teacher
trainer
waiter
writer

Agents ending in
er *spelled* **or**
actor
author
conductor
director
doctor
editor
janitor
mayor

sculptor
senator
sponsor
survivor
tailor
visitor

Other words end-
ing in **er** *spelled*
or
equator
major
minor
mirror
motor
numerator
transistor
American spelling
of words with **or**
color
harbor
honor
humor
labor
neighbor
vapor

Words ending
in **er** spelled **ar**
cellar
dollar
hangar
pillar
regular
sugar

Words with **er**
spelled **ir**
bird
dirt
firm
first
girl
shirt
third
whirl

Words with **er**
spelled **ur**
burn
curl
curve
hurt
nurse
purse
turn
urn

UNIT 17:
Long **ar** and **er**

Words with
long **ar** spelled
are
bare
care
rare
share
stare

Words with
long **ar** spelled
air
air
chair
fair
hair
pair
stair

Words with
long **er** spelled
ear
ear
clear
dear
fear
hear
near

Words with
long **er** spelled
eer
cheer
deer
peer
queer
steer

UNIT 18:
Vowel Sounds
ow, oy

Words with **ow**
spelled **ow**
brow
cow
how
now
wow
own
clown
crown
down

gown
town

Words with **ow**
spelled **ou**
out
about
pout
shout
stout
trout
ound
found
ground
pound
sound
round

Words with **oy**
spelled **oy**
boy
joy
Roy
soy
toy

Words with **oy**
spelled **oi**
oil
boil
broil
foil
soil
toil

UNIT 19:

Vowel Sound
oo as in *book*
ook
book
cook
look
shook
took
ood
good
hood
stood
wood

UNIT 20:

Words with the
letters **ie** and **ei**
Long **e** spelled
ie
belief
believe
chief
field
fierce
piece
niece
yield
shield

… except after c
ceiling
conceit
conceive
deceit
deceive
receive
receipt

… or when it
says long a
eight
eighteen
eighty
neighbour
rein
reign
sleigh
veil
vein
weigh
weight

Exceptions **to**
the ie "rule."
either
foreign
leisure
neither
sheik
weird

UNIT 22:

Compound
Words
birthplace
blueprint
bookkeeper
cardboard

carefree
daylight
doughnut
earring
everyone
extraordinary
farewell
fireproof
flashlight
forehead
frostbite
glowworm
haircut
hitchhike
homework
jackknife
loudspeaker
marshmallow
meanwhile
nevertheless
newspaper
nighttime
otherwise
overseas
paperback
pineapple
rattlesnake
roommate
safeguard
sideburns
sidewalk
skateboard
skyscraper
snowmobile
somebody
suitcase
teammate
teenage
throughout
toothbrush
typewriter
upright
uproar
viewpoint
volleyball
wastebasket
whatever
windshield
withhold

ADDING ENDINGS

UNIT 23:
Dropping e when adding ed or ing

admire	admired	admiring
advise	advised	advising
approve	approved	approving
argue	argued	arguing
arrange	arranged	arranging
arrive	arrived	arriving
become		becoming
choose		choosing
continue	continued	continuing
desire	desired	desiring
encourage	encouraged	encouraging
excuse	excused	excusing
guide	guided	guiding
hire	hired	hiring
hope	hoped	hoping
propose	proposed	proposing
rise		rising
scare	scared	scaring
scribble	scribbled	scribbling
separate	separated	separating
shine		shining
smuggle	smuggled	smuggling
solve	solved	solving
tackle	tackled	tackling
tease	teased	teasing
use	used	using
value	valued	valuing
wave	waved	waving

UNIT 24:
One Syllable Doubling Final Consonant when adding -ed or -ing

clog	clogged	clogging
cram	crammed	cramming
fit	fitted	fitting
flip	flipped	flipping
jut	jutted	jutting
map	mapped	mapping
rob	robbed	robbing
slam	slammed	slamming
slip	slipped	slipping

UNIT 25:
Changing y to i

clumsy	clumsiness
costly	costliest
dizzy	dizziness
duty	dutiful
empty	emptiness

envy	envious
fancy	fanciful
fury	furious
gloomy	gloomiest
greedy	greediness
heavy	heavily
hungry	hungrily
lucky	luckily
magnify	magnified
mercy	merciful
merry	merrily
modify	modified
mystery	mysterious
pity	pitiful
plenty	plentiful
steady	steadily
worthy	worthiness

UNIT 26:
Adding ly

absolute	absolutely
appropriate	appropriately
brave	bravely
close	closely
complete	completely
entire	entirely
extreme	extremely
immediate	immediately
infinite	infinitely
late	lately
like	likely
pure	purely
safe	safely
severe	severely
sincere	sincerely

UNITS 27, 28:
Plural Forms

compasses
glasses
octopuses
surpluses
eyelashes
beaches
branches
scratches
speeches
prefixes
reflexes
saxes
suffixes
alleys
attorneys

chimneys
donkeys
kidneys
monkeys
pulleys
turkeys
allies
assemblies
cities
countries
diaries
dairies
juries
libraries
luxuries
pastries
policies
skies
territories
theories
trophies
banjos
dynamos
memos
patios
photos
pianos
rodeos
studios
tacos
chiefs
dwarfs
handkerchiefs
roofs
scarfs
wharfs
elves
halves
leaves
lives
loaves
selves
shelves
thieves
wives

UNIT 30:
Contractions

hadn't	had not
hasn't	has not
haven't	have not
he'd	he would, he had
here's	here is
mustn't	must not
she'd	she would, she had

shouldn't	should not
they'll	they will
you'd	you would, you had
they'd	they had, they would
you've	you have
where's	where is
who's	who is

UNIT 31:
Homonyms

bare	bear
base	bass
board	bored
border	boarder
break	brake
chilly	chili
course	coarse
died	dyed
fair	fare
forth	fourth
fir	fur
great	grate
hanger	hangar
heard	herd
main	mane
pail	pale
pain	pane
pair	pare, pear
pore	pour
rain	reign
scent	sent, cent
some	sum
steak	stake
stationery	stationary
there	their
to	two, too
vain	vein
wait	weight
ware	wear
week	weak

UNIT 32:
Two or More Syllables
Stress on first syllable

benefit	benefited	benefiting
differ	differed	differing
happen	happened	happening
honour	honoured	honouring
listen	listened	listening
pardon	pardoned	pardoning
pilot	piloted	piloting
profit	profited	profiting

Stress on second syllable

acquit	acquitted	acquitting
commit	committed	committing
confer	conferred	conferring
control	controlled	controlling
expel	expelled	expelling
forbid		forbidding
omit	omitted	omitting
patrol	patrolled	patrolling
prefer	preferred	preferring
propel	propelled	propelling
refer	referred	referring
regret	regretted	regretting
repel	repelled	repelling

UNIT 34:
Related Words

Long or Short Vowel to Schwa

admire	admiration
confer	conference
define	definition
divide	dividend
fatal	fatality
habit	habitat
harmony	harmonious
history	historical
major	majority
narrate	narrative
politics	political
popular	popularity
regular	regularity
reside	resident
stable	stability

UNIT 35:
Prefixes

transaction
transcontinental
transfer
transform
transfusion
transistor
transmit
transplant
unbearable
uncommon
undecided
uneducated
unexpected
unknown
unnecessary
unpopular

interaction
interchange
intercollegiate
intercom
interdependent
interject
interlocking
interplanetary
interpret
interracial
interrupt
intersection
interval
interview
subcommittee
subconscious
subcontractor
subdivide
subdue
subheading
subliminal
submerge
subnormal
subordinate
subsistence

UNIT 36:
Suffixes

bitterness
cheerfulness
consciousness
forgetfulness
friendliness
happiness
loneliness
seriousness
accomplishment
argument
equipment
entertainment
judgment
temperament
attraction
completion
construction
demonstration
direction
edition
ejection
exhibition
infection
inspection
invention
location

operation
production
situation
addition
composition
recognition
repetition
transition
decision
conclusion
erosion
explosion
invasion
obsession
persuasion
profession
provision
revision
television
transfusion

UNIT 37:
Word Origins

bagel	Yiddish
cafeteria	Spanish
coleslaw	Dutch
freckles	Old Norse
judo	Japanese
kindergarten	German
lilac	Persian
mattress	Arabic
moose	Algonquin
mortgage	French
nickel	German
nuisance	French
penguin	Welsh
robot	Czech
salad	French
shamrock	Irish
wicker	Swedish

UNIT 38:
Silent Letters

castle
fasten
hustle
listen
whistle
wrestle
often
soften
assign

design
gnaw
resign
sign
bomb
climb
comb
crumb
dumb
lamb
limb
numb
plumber
thumb
tomb
calm
palm
salmon
folk
stalk
yolk
knack
knapsack
knee
kneel
knife
knight
knitting
knob
knot
knuckle
wrestle
wrinkle

UNIT 40:
Misleading
Pronunciations

accidentally
adjust
budget
chocolate
corduroy
diamond
district
empty
environment
governor
library
literature
miniature
perform
probably
pumpkin
restaurant

sandwich
secretary
similarly
sophomore
strength
supposed
surprised
temperament

UNIT 41:
Confusing Word Pairs

advice	advise
affect	effect
alley	ally
bath	bathe
choose	chose
county	country
custom	costume
device	devise
empire	umpire
preceding	proceeding
recipe	receipt
trail	trial
weather	whether

Appendix III

Answers

UNIT 1

Putting the Secret to Work
1. 26, 5, 21
2. apple, umbrella, elephant, octopus, igloo
4. bat, bit, bin, box
5. tin, tan, tot
6. pet, pen, pat
7. Word Search:

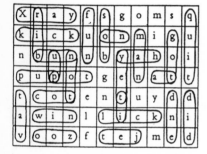

8. tan, run, sun, man
9. sit, sat, sip, set
10. dish, rash, wish, rush
11. rock, pick, luck, neck

UNIT 2

What's the Secret?
1. at
2. m<u>at</u>, s<u>at</u>, b<u>at</u>
3. Yes, they all end in **ug**.

Putting the Secret to Work
1. **at**—bat, cat, fat, hat, mat, pat, rat, sat, that;
   et—bet, get, jet, let, met, net, pet, vet, wet, yet;
   it—bit, fit, hit, kit, lit, pit, sit, wit, quit;
   ot—cot, dot, hot, jot, lot, not, pot, rot, shot;
   ut—cut, gut, nut, but
2. f<u>at</u>—c<u>at</u>, p<u>et</u>—g<u>et</u>, b<u>ut</u>—c<u>ut</u>, p<u>ot</u>—c<u>ot</u>

3. shut, ship, shop, shin
4. fat rat, wet jet, hot pot, flat hat
5. **ag**—bag, rag, sag, tag, wag, nag;
   eg—beg, leg, keg, peg;
   ig—big, dig, pig, fig, rig, wig;
   og—bog, dog, fog, hog, jog, log;
   ug—bug, dug, hug, mug, rug, tug
6. d<u>og</u>—fr<u>og</u>, b<u>eg</u>—l<u>eg</u>, r<u>ug</u>—t<u>ug</u>, r<u>ag</u>—b<u>ag</u>
7. frog, flag
8. job, cab, scrub
9. s<u>ob</u>, r<u>ob</u>, c<u>ub</u>, r<u>ub</u>, r<u>ib</u>, cr<u>ib</u>, s<u>ub</u>, club
10. 27, the, that
11. what

UNIT 3

What's the Secret?
1. h<u>ad</u>, d<u>ad</u>; <u>am</u> h<u>am</u>; <u>us</u>, b<u>us</u>
2. the sound of *z*

Putting the Secret to Work
1. **ad**—bad, dad, had, lad, mad, pad, sad, glad;
   id—bid, did, hid, kid, lid, rid, slid;
   ed—bed, fed, led, red, wed, sled;
   od—cod, god, nod, rod, sod;
   ud—bud, dud, mud, thud
2. glad dad, mad lad
3. said
4. bad—dad, bed—fed, nod—sod, bud—mud
5. **am**—dam, ham, jam, Sam, yam, slam;
   em—gem, hem, them;
   im—him, Jim, rim, slim, brim, swim
   um—gum, hum, mum, sum, drum, slum
6. from
7. dad, mom, Dad, Mom, Dad
8. them
9. **ends with s as in see:** us, this, gas, yes;

ends with z as in zip: was, as, has, his, does, is
10. was, as, as, this, His, is, does, has, us
11. bat, bus, bed, kid, log, jam

UNIT 4

What's the Secret?
1. **words ending in n:** an, run, fun, man;
   words ending in p: up, top, ship;
   words ending in x: fix, box, six
2. two, two

Putting the Secret to Work
1. **an**—ban, can, fan, man, pan, ran, tan, van, plan, than;
   en—den, hen, men, pen, ten, then, when;
   in—bin, din, fin, pin, tin, win, chin, grin, skin, spin, thin;
   un—bun, fun, gun, nun, pun, run, sun, spun
2. an—than, when—then, chin—spin
3. Use **an** before a vowel, **a** before a consonant: a bird, an ostrich, an animal, a lion, an insect, a mosquito
4. **ap**—cap, gap, lap, map, nap, rap, tap, chap, clap, slap, snap, trap, wrap, strap, scrap;
   ip—dip, hip, lip, nip, rip, sip, tip, zip, chip, clip, drip, flip, grip, ship, skip, slip, trip, whip, strip;
   ep—pep, step;
   op—cop, hop, mop, pop, top, chop, drop, shop, stop;
   up—cup, pup
5. ship, slip; trap, snap; cop, shop; chip, dip; skip, trip
6. **ax**—fax, Max, tax, wax;
   ex—sex, Rex
   ix—fix, mix, six;
   ox—box, fox;
   ux—tux

7. Max, fax, tax; fix, tux, six; fox, box
8. than, then, when; one, seven
9. seven, than, One, when, Then

UNIT 5

What's the Secret?
1. pi<u>tch</u>, ca<u>tch</u>, scra<u>tch</u>, wa<u>tch</u>
2. de<u>ck</u>, ne<u>ck</u>, che<u>ck</u>
3. be<u>st</u>, ne<u>st</u>, re<u>st</u>

Putting the Secret to Work
1. catch, pitch, scratch
2. **atch**—batch, catch, match, scratch, snatch;
   itch—hitch, ditch, pitch, glitch, stitch, switch, twitch;
   otch—notch, blotch, scotch;
   utch—Dutch, hutch, clutch, crutch
   which, much, such
3. watch
4. **ack**—back, pack, sack, tack, quack, shack, track;
   eck—deck, neck, check, speck, wreck;
   ick—lick, pick, sick, tick, brick, chick, quick, stick, trick;
   ock—dock, lock, rock, sock, block, o'clock, shock;
   uck—buck, duck, luck, puck, suck, tuck, stuck, truck
5. n<u>eck</u>—wr<u>eck</u>, t<u>ack</u>—bl<u>ack</u>, l<u>ick</u>—p<u>ick</u>, bl<u>ock</u>—cl<u>ock</u>
6. o'clock, truck, black, back, neck
7. **ast**—cast, fast, last, mast, past, vast, blast;
   est—best, nest, pest, rest, test, vest, west, zest, crest;
   ist—fist, list, mist, wrist;
   ost—cost, lost, frost;
   ust—bust, dust, gust, just, must, rust, crust, trust
8. best, cost, last
9. dish, fish; crash, dash; brush, blush
10. ask, desk, risk, dusk
11. Answers will vary.

UNIT 6

What's the Secret?
1. consonants are doubled
2. limp—chimp; jump—pump

Putting the Secret to Work
1. **ill**—bill, fill, hill, kill, mill, pill, till, will, chill, skill, spill, still;
   ell—bell, cell, fell, sell, tell, well, yell, spell, smell;
   all—ball, call, fall, hall, mall, wall, tall, small
2. pill—bill, mall—tall, sell—well, gull—dull
3. spell, well; will, call; fell
4. **ass**—bass, mass, pass, class, grass, glass;
   ess—less, mess, bless, chess, dress, guess, press, stress;
   oss—boss, loss, moss, cross, gloss, floss;
   iss—kiss, miss;
   uss—fuss, muss
5. chess, floss, glass
6. cuff, huff, stuff, bluff, fluff, gruff, scruff, scuff
7. If, of; If, of; If, of
8. off, off, of, of, of
9. Alps, scalp, help, gulp
10. half, until, saw
11. Word Search

UNIT 7

What's the Secret?
1. pi<u>nk</u>—thi<u>nk</u>, ri<u>ng</u>—thi<u>ng</u>, be<u>nt</u>—we<u>nt</u>
2. talk, friend, built

Putting the Secret to Work
1. **and**—band, hand, land, sand, stand, grand, brand;
   ing—king, ring, sing, wing, bring, swing, thing, sting, spring, string;
   ent—bent, cent, dent, lent, sent, tent, went, spent, scent;
   end—bend, send, spend, mend, trend, lend
2. long, find, want, end, and
3. and, end
4. went, want, went
5. **c sounds like s:** cent, city, cell, centre, circle;
   c sounds like k: cap, cup, car, cold, cut, cat
6. **ank**—bank, rank, sank, tank, yank, blank, drank, spank, thank, shrank;
   ink—link, mink, pink, rink, sink, wink, blink, drink, stink, think, shrink;
   unk—bunk, hunk, junk, sunk, drunk, skunk, stunk, trunk, shrunk
7. ya<u>nk</u>—bla<u>nk</u>, le<u>nt</u>—spe<u>nt</u>, ju<u>nk</u>—su<u>nk</u>
8. skunk, think, left, thank, skunk, next
9. cold, sold, gold
10. theft, gift, drift, shift
11. friend, built, talk, second, won

UNIT 8

What's the Secret?
3. mane, code, gape, note

Putting the Secret to Work
1. **ade**—fade, jade, made, wade, blade, glade, grade, spade, shade, trade;
   ake—bake, cake, fake, lake, make, quake, rake, sake, take, wake, brake, shake, flake, stake;
   ate—date, gate, hate, late, mate, fate, grate, slate, state;
   ace—face, lace, pace, race, brace, grace, place, space, trace;
   ame—came, fame, name, same, tame, game, blame, frame, flame, lame, shame
2. gave, wave; came, name; gate, late; quake, shake; race, place

3. have, short **a**
4. **ope**—cope, lope, hope, mope, rope, slope;
   oke—Coke, joke, poke, woke, broke, choke, spoke;
   ole—hole, mole, pole, role, sole, stole;
   ose—hose, nose, pose, rose, chose, those
5. come, some, done, love, gone
6. those, home, hole, woke, hope; Answer to riddle: smoke
7. mate, cane, gape, mane, rode, tape, robe, fade, note, fate, cape, globe

UNIT 9

What's the Secret?
1. ride, these
2. bite, ripe; The sound has become long **i**.

Putting the Secret to Work
1. ride—side, nice—slice, smile—while
2. **ice**—dice, mice, nice, rice, price, slice, spice, twice, vice;
   ide—hide, ride, side, tide, wide, bride, glide, guide, pride, slide, stride;
   ike—bike, dike, hike, mike, pike, like, spike, strike;
   ine—dine, fine, line, mine, nine, pine, shine, spine, swine, twine, wine, whine;
   ite—bite, kite, quite, write, spite, sprite, site, white
3. nine, ride, bike; like, nice, white, kite; write
4. **ime**—time, lime, chime, crime, dime, prime, slime;
   ive—dive, five, hive, live, drive, strive;
   ile—mile, pile, tile, smile, while;
   ipe—pipe, ripe, wipe, swipe, stripe;
   ife—life, wife, knife, strife
5. live
6. awhile, five, life, pipe, time, while
7. complete, these; some times, a while

UNIT 10

What's the Secret?
1. she, tree, eat
2. pretty, behind, many

Putting the Secret to Work
1. be, She, He, We, me
2. **ee**—bee, see, fee, knee, tree, free
3. see, tree
4. **eed**—deed, feed, weed, seed, breed, greed, bleed, speed;
   eek—meek, seek, week, creek, cheek, sleek;
   eel—feel, heel, kneel, peel, reel, steel, wheel;
   een—been, keen, seen, green, queen, screen;
   eep—beep, deep, peep, weep, cheep, creep, sheep, sleep, steep;
   eet—beet, feet, meet, fleet, greet, sheet, sleet
5. **e, e;**
   eak—beak, freak, leak, peak, weak, bleak;
   eal—deal, heal, meal, peal, seal, real, steal;
   eam—beam, cream, dream, gleam, team, steam, scream;
   ean—bean, clean, jean, lean, mean;
   each—teach, reach, bleach, peach, beach;
   eat—beat, meat, neat, seat, cheat, treat, wheat
6. weak, week; bee, be; meet, meat
7. teach, eat
8. Word Search

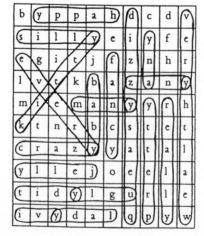

9. key
10. really, behind, began, radio, every

UNIT 11

What's the Secret?
1. long **a**
2. Yes
3. may•be, al•ways, a•fraid, a•gain

Putting the Secret to Work
1. bay, day, ray, way, clay, hay, may, pay, play; lay, jay, stay, tray, say, gray, stray; Answer to the riddle: before calculators
2. stay, always, maybe, okay, away
3. birthday, Sunday, Monday, Tuesday, Wednesday, Thursday, Friday, Saturday, holiday
4. **ail**—bail, fail, hail, jail, mail, nail, pail, rail, sail, wail;
   ain—gain, lain, main, pain, rain, vain, brain, chain, grain, plain, stain, strain;
   aid—paid, laid, braid, raid
5. straight, afraid, again, brain, wait, paint, tail
6. again
7. they, straight
8. great, steak, break; No

UNIT 12

What's the Secret?
1. **i:** tiger, sign, island;
   igh: might, fight, high;
   y: why, my, sky, myself
2. No, these spellings are used at the end or in the middle of words.

Putting the Secret to Work
1. **y**—by, my, cry, dry, fly, shy, sky, sly, spy, try, why
2. why, my, sky, try, by, reply
3. myself
4. fight, light, might, night, right, sight, tight, bright, fright, flight, plight, slight
5. high
6. night, right, fight, might, right; right was used twice, Answer to the riddle: thigh
7. pie, tie, die, lie

8. tiger, Irish island, tiny, ivy
9. sign, b<u>uys</u>, goodb<u>ye</u>, <u>eye</u>, i<u>s</u>land
10. sign, buys, eye, goodbye
11. eye, bye
12. by, buy, by, Bye, by

UNIT 13

What's the Secret?
1. long **o**, yes
2. the letter **o**; <u>o</u>•pen, <u>o</u>•ver, <u>on</u>•ly, <u>al</u>•so, hell•<u>o</u>, a•<u>go</u>
3. ow

Putting the Secret to Work
1. **o**—so, go, no;
   oat—coat, goat, moat, bloat, float, throat;
   ow—bow, low, row, tow, mow, blow, glow, grow, crow, show, slow, snow, stow, throw, know, flow
2. ago, boat, only, road, so, go, open, boat, over, also, Hello, throw, Oh, no, old
3. toad, load; goat, float, coat
4. going, gone, goes, went, go
5. goes, almost, know, though, ocean; Answer to riddle: A glue stick
6. Responses will vary
7. No; know; Know, no; no, know
8. almost, ocean; ocean

UNIT 14

What's the Secret?
1. bl<u>ue</u>, s<u>oon</u>, t<u>oo</u>
2. Answers will vary

Putting the Secret to Work
1. to—in the direction of; too—also, more than enough; two—one more than one
   two; to; two;too; to; to; two; to
2. **oon**—goon, soon, moon, loon, spoon, balloon;
   oom—boom, doom, room, zoom, broom, gloom, groom;
   oot—boot, hoot, loot, root, toot, scoot, shoot;
   ool—cool, fool, pool, tool, drool, school, spool, stool;
   oop—coop, hoop, loop, droop, scoop, snoop, troop

3. **ute**—flute, brute, cute;
   use—fuse, muse, amuse;
   ude—dude, nude, rude;
   uge—huge, refuge;
   ule—rule, mule, yule
4. huge, cute
5. dew, few, mew, new, pew, jew, grew, knew, blew, stew, screw, threw
6. knew; new
7. Do, you; New, blue; You, too; few, soon, new; Use, to
8. glue, blue, clue, true, cue
9. fruit, suit, bruise, cruise, juice; fruit, bruise, juice; suit, cruise
10. who, do, to, into
11. in, into, into, into, in, into

UNIT 15

What's the Secret?
1. different
2. **o** becomes **or**
3. f<u>or</u>, y<u>our</u>, r<u>oar</u>, m<u>ore</u>, c<u>our</u>t

Putting the Secret to Work
1. start—cart, hard—yard, fort—short
2. **ar**—bar, car, far, jar, par, tar, scar, star;
   ark—bark, dark, hark, lark, mark, park, shark;
   art—Bart, dart, part, tart, start, chart
3. **arm**—farm, harm, charm;
   ard—guard, hard, yard;
   arch—March, starch, march;
   arp—carp, harp, sharp;
   arge—charge, barge, large
4. park, shark, farm, March; park, farm, March, shark; Answer to riddle: An arch
5. **ore**—bore, core, gore, more, pore, sore, store, score, snore, chore;
   ort—port, fort, sort, short, snort, sport
6. **orm**—storm, form, Norm;
   our—four, pour, your;
   oar—soar, roar, boar;
   orn—born, torn, worn
7. door, floor
8. your, roar, board, store, morning, door, four, more
9. warm, war, are, heart, before
10. warm, heart, are, war, before;

Answer to riddle: wharf
11. for, for, four, for, four

UNIT 16

What's the Secret?
1. The vowel sound changes a bit.
2. **er**
3. The sound is spelled differently.

Putting the Secret to Work
1. bird, girl, water, first
2. worm, work, world, worse, worth, worst
3. her, turn, surprise, after, better, ever, never, doctor, purple
4. turn, surprise, better, after, doctor, never, her, purple, ever
5. singer, player, worker, teacher, waiter
6. heard, were, dollars, learn, birthday
7. heard, learn, were, birthday, dollars
8. Word Search

UNIT 17

What's the Secret?
1. **ear**—fear, year;
   ere—here, sphere;
   eer—steer, beer
2. the letter **e**
3. the letter **i**

Putting the Secret to Work
1. **ear**—dear, fear, gear, hear, near, rear, tear, clear, spear;
   eer—beer, deer, peer, queer, steer, sheer

151

2. clear, cheer, ear, here, years, appear
3. Here, here, hear, hear; dear, deer, dear
4. **are**—bare, care, dare, fare, mare, rare, scare, share, spare, square, stare, hare;
   air—fair, pair, hair, stair, chair
5. fare—fair; hare—hair; stares—stairs
6. where, their, there, very, marry
7. There, their; Their, there; There, their
8. Responses will vary.
9. **arry**—marry, Harry, carry

UNIT 18

What's the Secret?
1. br<u>ow</u>n, t<u>ow</u>n, g<u>ow</u>n; ab<u>ou</u>t sh<u>ou</u>t, c<u>ou</u>nt
2. oy; j<u>oi</u>n, c<u>oi</u>n, s<u>oi</u>l, t<u>oi</u>l, v<u>oi</u>ce, ch<u>oi</u>ce

Putting the Secret to Work
1. **ow**—bow, cow, how, now, pow, wow, brow, plow;
   own—down, gown, town, clown, crown;
   out—about, pout, shout, trout;
   ound—bound, found, mound, pound, ground, sound, around
2. owl; howl, scowl, prowl, growl
3. mouse; house, louse, grouse
4. out, now, our, down, around, hour, brown, found, house, how; Answer to rhyme: How now brown cow?
5. our, hour
6. **oil**—boil, foil, soil, toil, broil, spoil;
   oy—boy, joy, soy, toy, annoy, employ
7. join, voice, noise
8. join, noise, annoy; boy, soil, voice
9. without, outside
10. outburst, outcast, outside, outfield, outlet, outdoors, outfit

UNIT 19

What's the Secret?
1. u̇, ou
2. u̇, ou (the gh is silent)
3. o

Putting the Secret to Work
1. **ook**—book, cook, hook, look, nook, took, brook, crook, shook;
   ood—good, hood, wood, stood
2. **oo as in took**: brook, good, wood, shook;
   oo as in tune: pool, zoo, boom, zoom, soon, too, stool, food
3. took, look, book; push, put, good looking
4. ou, l; would, could, should
5. ou, gh
6. mother, father, brother, sister, daughter, son
7. mother, father; brother
8. Responses will vary.
9. caught, another, months, enough
10. taught, teach, catch, caught

UNIT 20

What's the Secret?
1. **ie pronounced long e**: field, piece, niece, thief, yield, movie, believe;
   ei pronounced long a: vein, weigh, eight, neighbour
2. ei; c; r<u>ec</u>eive, d<u>ec</u>eive, c<u>eil</u>ing, conc<u>ei</u>ted

Putting the Secret to Work
1. thief, field, believe, piece, yield, fierce, niece; yes
2. receive, receipt, ceiling, deceive, deceit, conceit; yes
3. receive—take something, be given; ceiling—the top covering of a room; conceit—too much pride in oneself; receipt—a written statement that money, or a letter was received; deceive—make someone believe something untrue
4. vein, neighbour's; weigh; eight
5. neighbour, eight, weigh, vein; yes
6. either, neither, height, seize
7. science, seize, neither, either, height
8. science

UNIT 21

What's the Secret?
1. 2 syllables: bottom, machine,

police, squirrel;
3 syllables: animals, discover, family, hospital, pollution, suddenly, together, beautiful, equipment, finishing, dinosaur (vegetable, interesting);
more than 3 syllables: television, everybody, situation (vegetable, interesting)
2. vegetable, interesting
3. a) di´•no•saur
   b) to•geth´•er
   c) ma•chine´

Putting the Secret to Work
1. a) pol•lu•tion
   b) tel•e•vi•sion
   c) dis•cov•er
2. a) beautiful
   b) interesting
   c) everybody
   d) vegetable
3. a) squirrel
   b) television
4. a) machine, police
   b) discover, pollution, together, equipment
5. suddenly, squirrel, pollution, bottom

UNIT 22

What's the Secret?
1. carload, carwash, carport; because there is a logical connection between the meaning of the small words and the compound word.
2. bookkeeper = book + keeper
   granddaughter= grand + daughter
   nighttime= night + time
   hitchhike= hitch + hike

Putting the Secret to Work
1. playground, headache, firefighter
2. a) breakfast: to end a fast (a time of not eating)
   b) kindergarten: garden of children (German)
   c) cupboard: a shelf or board where cups are kept
3. anywhere, nowhere, anyone, somewhere, someone, sometime, anything, nothing, everywhere, everything, everyone
4. a) earthquake

b) bookkeeper
c) headache
5. a) every day
   b) everyday
   c) everyday
   d) every day

UNIT 23

What's the Secret?
1. a) having—have, driving—drive, coming—come, learned—learn, laughed—laugh, watching—watch
   b) e
2. a) fired; b) frightened; c) exciting; d) listening
3. listened, practised, screamed, surrounded, decided, learned
4. had, wrote, drove

Putting the Secret to Work
1. a) listening, noisy; b) decided, laughing, watching; c) frightened, scary
2. a) rough; b) cough; c) tough; d) enough

UNIT 24

What's the Secret?
1. a) blur, swim, fun, spot, knit, fog; b) the final consonant of the base word is doubled
2. striped—stripe, stripped—strip, scared—scare, scarred—scar
   Base words ending in e: the "e" is dropped and "ed" is added; base words ending in a vowel and consonant: the final consonant is doubled; ed is added.

Putting the Secret to Work
1. a) stopped, stopping;
   b) blurred, blurring, blurry;
   c) stepped, stepping;
   d) winning;
   e) fogged, fogging, foggy
2. a) stripped, striped; b) scared, scarred
3. a) rob; b) yap; c) grab; d) map; e) edge; f) operate; g) erase; h) tame. Answer: geometry
4. climb, crumb, dumb, womb, tomb, thumb, numb, comb, limb, lamb, bomb, jamb

UNIT 25

What's the Secret?
1. a) no change; b) y changed to i
2. glorious—glory, various—vary, mysterious—mystery

Putting the Secret to Work
1. a) funniest; b) qualified, supplied; c) worrying, glorious, friendliness; d) mysterious, denying; e) buried, tried, worried
2. furious, mysterious, studious, envious, glorious, luxurious, various
3. funniest, happiness, occupied, supplied, worried, classified, hurried, married
4. friend, friends, friendly, friendliness, friendship, friendless, befriend, befriended, unfriendly, friendlier, friendliest

UNIT 26

What's the Secret?
1. careful, awful, final, continual, actual
2. a) surely, actively, politely, rarely, loosely, entirely, closely, likely, lively
3. a) terribly, horribly, responsibly, comfortably, fashionably
4. a) angry, happy, steady

Putting the Secret to Work
1. a) busily, lazily; b) easily, luckily; c) noisily, clumsily, hungrily
2. a) continually; b) certainly; c) probably; d) quietly; e) lonely; f) truly
3. Answers will vary

UNIT 27

What's the Secret?
1. a) circus, guess, toothbrush, speech, mailbox; add -es
2. heroes, radios, mosquitoes, pianos, videos, tomatoes

Putting the Secret to Work
1. searches, astronauts, noses, dishes, waxes, iguanas, campuses, hoaxes, echoes, sopranos
2. a) tomatoes; b) mosquitoes; c) toothbrushes; d) skis; d) pianos
3. guesses, businesses, scratches, pictures, languages, circuses, sandwiches, addresses, illnesses
4. The acts are performed in a large ring; a three ring circus.

UNIT 28

What's the Secret?
1. A: end in vowel + y; B: end in consonant + y. In A, the plural is formed by adding s; in B, the y is changed to i and es is added.

Putting the Secret to Work
1. a) monkeys, babies;
   b) surveys, cavities;
   c) journeys, countries
2. a) diagnoses; b) hypotheses; c) data
3. a) 3; b) 5; c) 4; d) 1; e) 2
4. a) a century is one **hundred** years;
   b) a cent is one one-**hundred**th of a dollar;
   c) bicentennial means two **hundred** years;
   d) a centimetre is one one-**hundred**th of a metre

UNIT 29

What's the Secret?
1. a) goalie's; b) dress's; c) editor's; d) school's
2. a) goalies'; b) dresses'; c) editors'; d) schools'
3. a) men's; b) women's; c) people's

Putting the Secret to Work
1. a) Houses; b) guitar's, cousins; c) babies', parents
2. a) the men's bicycles;
   b) the women's racquets;
   c) the people's opinions;
   d) the deer's antlers
   Other combinations are possible.
3. a) guilty; b) fatigue; c) guide; d) tongue; e) disguise

UNIT 30

What's the Secret?
1. a) one letter removed: didn't, wasn't, what's, there's, I'm, you're, it's, let's, that's, don't, wouldn't, we're, doesn't, they're, weren't,
    more than one letter removed: they've, we'd, it'll, can't

Putting the Secret to Work
1. a) We'd, they've; b) Here's, don't, we've; c) doesn't, you're, won't
2. a) Who's; b) When's; c) What's; d) How's

3. they've, they're, she's, I'm, I've, he's, you've, you're, hasn't, haven't, isn't, aren't, shouldn't, couldn't, wouldn't, doesn't
4. a) It's, its; b) it's, its; c) its, it's
5. a) you're, your; b) your, you're

UNIT 31

What's the Secret
1. a) We saw the kitten **pause** as she **passed** the doorway. Suddenly she **threw** herself at a ball of wool she had **seen** on the chair.
    b) Our Family Studies teacher never **allowed** us to **waste flour** when we were baking.
    c) The **principal** wanted us to know **whose lead** pencil was stuck in the lock.

Putting the Secret to Work
1. a) cheap; b) be; c) choose; d) wait; e) sale
2. The <u>past</u> few <u>hours</u> have been a complete <u>waste</u> of time. I wasn't <u>allowed</u> to go to Shane's until I weeded the <u>flower</u> beds. Then my dog walked <u>through</u> the house with mud all over his <u>paws</u>.
    I had never <u>seen</u> such a mess! I <u>led</u> him out to his doghouse, and <u>who's</u> <u>there</u>? My little brother playing in the same puddle!
4. a) A bare bear; b) A bored board;

c) A fair fare; d) A minor miner; e) A hare's hair; f) stationary stationery

UNIT 32

What's the Secret?
1. First syllable is stressed. No changes are made to the base word.
    a) pardoned—pardoning, listened—listening, profited—profiting
2. The final syllable is stressed; the final consonant is doubled when -ed and -ing are added.
    a) expelled—expelling, transmitted—transmitting, controlled—controlling

Putting the Secret to Work
1. a) forgetting; b) blanketed; c) beginning; d) committed; e) reasoning
2. a) opportunity; b) multiplication; c) necessary; d) temperature e) immediately
3. a) successful, occurred, immediately, necessary, opportunity; d) special

UNIT 33

What's the Secret?
1. college, capital, minute, pleasant, lettuce, engine
2. a) recommend; b) compliment; c) horrible; d) guarantee

Putting the Secret to Work
1. a) bargain; b) certain; c) curtain; d) villain; e) captain; f) mountain; g) fountain
2. a) Vancouver; b) Toronto; c) Montreal; d) Victoria
3. a) ban<u>qu</u>et, n<u>ui</u>sance, <u>gu</u>arantee
    b) co<u>ll</u>ege, le<u>tt</u>uce, ho<u>rr</u>ible, reco<u>mm</u>end, po<u>ss</u>ible, a<u>cc</u>ident

UNIT 34

What's the Secret?
1. a) response; b) origin; c) depend; d) history

2. a) confident—confide; b) invitation—invite; c) competition—compete; d) composition—compose

Putting the Secret to Work
1. a) muscular; b) resignation; c) bombard; d) condemnation
2. a) photographer; b) photography; c) photographic; d) photograph
3. a) musician; b) politician; c) mathematician; d) physician; e) cosmetician; f) electrician; g) beautician; h) dietician; i) technician

UNIT 35

What's the Secret?
1. a) unnatural; b) disrespectful; c) unfortunately; d) unconscious; e) disappear; f) discontinued; g) unpredictable; h) disagreeable
2. transport, import, export, deport, report, transports, transported, transporting, transportation, imports, imported, importer, importing, exports, exported, exporter, exporting, deports, deported, deporting, deportation

Putting the Secret to Work
1. a) description; b) inscription; c) subscriptions; d) prescription
2. a) international; b) interplanetary; c) interprovincial; d) intercollegiate
3. a) Latin; b) money; c) ore; d) rest

UNIT 36

What's the Secret?
1. a) requirement; b) carelessness; c) harassment; d) nervousness
2. a) conclusion; b) admission; c) imagination; d) division
3. a) competition—compete; b) definition—define; c) opposition—oppose; d) repetition—repeat

Putting the Secret to Work
1. a) awareness; b) carelessness;

c) forgiveness; d) nervousness;
e) laziness
3. comparison, comparable;
progressive, progression;
profession, professor; predictable,
prediction, predictor

UNIT 37

What's the Secret?
1. a) French: limousine, caterpillar,
cashier
b) Greek: ozone, crystal, sarcasm
c) Spanish: tornado, barbecue
d) Dutch: knuckle, yacht
e) Arabic: coffee, syrup
f) German: pretzel, snorkel
g) American Indian: moccasin,
raccoon
h) Old Norse: reindeer
i) West African: banana
j) Chinese: typhoon
k) Latin: schedule

Putting the Secret to Work
1. a) yacht; b) typhoon; c) crystal;
d) syrup; e) pretzel; f) knuckle
2. a) coffee; b) raccoon; c) moccasin;
d) caterpillar
4. a) limousine; b) cashier;
c) reindeer; d) barbecue
5. a) toboggan: from Algonquian
"tobakun" (handsled)
b) malaria: from Italian:
"malaaria" (bad air)
c) chipmunk: from Algonquian:
means "headfirst" (refers to the
chipmunk's way of going down a
tree trunk)

UNIT 38

What's the Secret
2. a) column—columnist;
b) autumn—autumnal;
c) condemn—condemnation
3. a) doubt; b) vehicle;
c) pumpkin; d) debt; e) mortgage;
f) daughter

Putting the Secret to Work
1. a) knuckle; b) known; c) knife;
d) knead; e) knight; f) knob
g) knotty
Answer: Lettuce in and you'll
find out!
2. a) receipt; b) foreign; c) jealous;
d) vacuum

UNIT 39

Putting the Secret to Work
1. a) appointment; b) village;
c) official; d) exaggerate;
e) stubborn; f) sufficient;
g) rabbit; h) suggestion
2. a) blizzard; b) hurricane;
c) interrupt; d) accidentally;
e) terrific; f) irrigation;
g) occasion; h) possession;
i) marriage; j) tomorrow;
k) dilemma
4. a) accident; b) appoint; c) suggest;
d) irrigate; e) possess; f) suffice

UNIT 40

Putting the Secret to Work
1. a) pronunciation; b) particularly;
c) valuable; d) laboratory
3. a) exception; b) exceptional;
c) exceptionally
4. real—really, reality, realism,
realize, realization, realistic,
realist, unreal, unrealistic,
realistically
6. a) lightning; b) raspberry;
c) depth; d) length; e) adjective

UNIT 41

What's the Secret?
1. a) angel, angle; b) breath, breathe;
c) close, clothes; d) dairy, diary;
e) desert, dessert; f) loose, lose;
g) rhyme, rhythm; h) accept,
except; i) personnel, personal;
j) quite, quiet

Putting the Secret to Work
2. a) diary; b) dairy; c) angel;
d) angle; e) quiet; f) quite;
g) except; h) accept

3. acceptance, acceptable,
exception, exceptional

UNIT 42

Putting the Secret to Work
1. pageant, soldier, restaurant, feud,
tortoise, lieutenant, cocoa, canoe
3. a) diamond, miniature,
parliament
b) biscuit, circuit, penguin
(any order)
c) Tuesday, rescue, tongue
d) leopard, surgeon

Recommended Resources

Other Books on Spelling by the Authors

Scott, Ruth, and Siamon, Sharon. *The Canadian Spelling Program II*, Grades 2-6. Toronto: Gage Educational Publishing Company.
    A series of spelling texts for Grades 2 to 6

Scott, Ruth. *Spelling: Sharing the Secrets*. Toronto: Gage Educational Publishing Company. 1993.
    A professional text prepared for teachers on the teaching of spelling. Contains many examples of how to teach spelling throughout the schoolday.

Scott, Ruth. *The Student Editor's Guide to Words*. Toronto: Gage Educational Publishing Company, 1991.
    A resource containing a wealth of information about English spelling including rules, word families, spelling strategies, and supporting lists.

Word Games

Golick, Margie. *Playing with Words*. Markham, Ontario: Pembroke Books, 1987.

Maestro, G. *Too Hot to Hoot: Funny Palindrome Riddles*. New York: Houghton Mifflin Co., 1985. (Distributed in Canada by Thomas Allen & Son, Toronto.)

_____, *What's a Frank Frank? Tasty Homograph Riddles*. New York: Houghton Mifflin Co., 1985. (Distributed in Canada by Thomas Allen & Son, Toronto.)

Moscovitch, R. *What's in a Word? A Dictionary of Daffy Definitions*. Boston: Houghton Mifflin Co., 1985. (Distributed in Canada by Thomas Allen & Son, Toronto.)

Terban, M. *Hey, Hay! A Wagonful of Funny Homonym Riddles*. New York: Houghton Mifflin Co., 1985. (Distributed in Canada by Thomas Allen & Son, Toronto.)

Glossary

adverb:
a word that extends or limits the meaning of *verbs* (She sings **well.**), *adjectives* (You speak **very** clearly.), or *other adverbs* (I am **very** tired.)

base word:
a word to which prefixes, suffixes, or other affixes can be added: **nation**, **nation**al, inter**nation**al

blend:
a blend is a speech sound made when two consonants are said together as in *bl, cl* or *gr.*

compound word:
a word made by joining together two or more separate words: **baseball, highway**

consonant:
a speech sound made by completely or partly blocking the breath, such as **b**, **t**, and **d**. All the letters of the alphabet that are not vowels are consonants.

contraction:
a shortened form of two words: **could not—couldn't**; **will not— won't**

homonym (homophone):
one of two or more words having the same pronunciation but different meanings, origins, and spellings: **wrote—rote**; **its—it's**

long vowel sound:
a vowel sound is long if the letter says its own name. The long vowels are *a* as in *ate*, *e* as in *eat*, *i* as in *ice*, *o* as in *open*, *u* as in *use*.

mnemonic device:
an aid to memory: the princi**pal** is your **pal**

noun:
a word used as the name of a person, place, thing, quality, or event: **Carlo** showed great **happiness** when the **present** at his **party** turned out to be a new **bike**.

past tense:
in grammar, a verb that expresses an action that happened or a condition that existed in time gone by: I **went** to the movies last night. She **ran** the race yesterday.

plural:
a form of a word to show that it means more than one: several **books**

possessive:
the form of a noun or pronoun that shows possession or ownership: **the boy's books** (the books belonging to a boy), **the girls' trophies** (the trophies belonging to the girls)

prefix:
a syllable or word put at the beginning of a word to change its meaning or to form a new word: **pre**paid, **sub**way

pun:
a humorous use of a word where it can have different meanings: Humpty Dumpty had a great fall, but the winter was rough.

rhyme:
two words rhyme when they sound the same at the end: *fit, pit.*

rhyming family:
words in rhyming families sound the same at the end, and are spelled with the same pattern: *cat, fat, hat, mat.*

schwa vowel:
an unstressed vowel sound such as that of the *a* in *about*, the *u* in *circus*, or the *o* in *lemon*. The symbol used to represent this sound is ə.

short vowel sound:
the short vowel sounds are *a* as in *at*, *e* as in *end*, *i* as in *it*, *o* as in *on*, *u* as in *up*.

singular:
referring to one only

stressed syllable:
a greater degree of force or loudness given to a certain syllable in a word; a mark to show a stressed syllable: fam´ i ly.

suffix:
a syllable or syllables put at the end of a word to form another word: good**ness**, spoon**ful**, amaze**ment**

syllable:
a word or part of a word spoken as a unit, usually consisting of a vowel alone or a vowel sound with one or more consonant sounds: syl•la•ble

verb:
a word that expresses an action or state of being: **run**, **work**, **understand**.

vowel:
a speech sound in which the breath is not stopped at any point by the teeth, tongue, or lips. When you say *ah* you are saying a vowel. The letters that spell vowels are **a**, **e**, **i**, **o**, **u** and sometimes **y**.

vowel combination:
two vowels together making one sound, as in *pool, road.*

DICTATION WORKSHEET

DICTATION	REWRITE	POSTTEST